Briefings,

The Essential

Diagrams

Copyright Lulu Author Bill Bryans
ISBN 978-1-4452-6355-7

Introduction
ADI Part 3 Preset tests

Test 1

Beginner controls & (If there is time) Moving Off / Stopping

Crossroads

Test 2

Moving Off/Stopping

Meet, Cross and Overtake, Keep a Safe Distance, Adequate Distance, Anticipation

Test 3

Turn in the Road

Junctions Major to Minor

Test 4 (a & b)

Reversing Left or Right

T junctions when Emerging

Test 5

Emergency stop/ The Correct use of Mirrors &Mirror Vision

The Correct use of Speed and Correct road Positioning

Test 6

Pedestrian Crossings/The Correct use of Signals both by Arm & Indicator

Reverse Parking

Test 7

Junctions Major to Minor

Pedestrian crossings/The Correct use of Signals both by Arm & Indicator

Test 8

T Junctions when Emerging

Meet Cross and Overtake, Keep a Safe Distance, Adequate Distance, Anticipation

Test 9

Crossroads

Pedestrian Crossings/The Correct use of Signals both by Arm & Indicator

Test 10

Meet Cross and Overtake, Keep a Safe Distance, Adequate Distance, Anticipation

The Correct use of Speed and Correct Road Positioning

Content Index

Part 1	The Controls Lesson	4
Part 2	Moving Off & Stopping	13
Part 3	Straight Reversing	20
Part 4	Turn in the Road	22
Part 5	Reverse to the Left	25
Part 6	Reverse to the Right	28
Part 7	Reverse Park	31
Part 8 a	Emergency Stop	40
Part 8 b	Correct use of Mirrors & Mirror Vision	34
Part 9	Junctions Major to Minor	45
Part 10	'T' Junctions when Emerging	50
Part 11	Crossroads	56
Part 12 a	Meet Approaching Traffic	65
Part 12 b	Allow Adequate Clearance to Stationary Hazards	68
Part 12 c	Keep a Safe Distance	70 -71
Part 12 d	Anticipation of Pedestrians, Cyclist, Drivers & Animals	**69, 71,** 72
Part 13	Cut Across Approaching Traffic	73
Part 14	Overtaking	78
Part 15	Pedestrian Crossings	87
Part 16	Signals by both Arm & Indicator – School Crossing Warden	94
Part 17	Roundabouts	96

Preset Test 1

The Controls Lesson

Doors

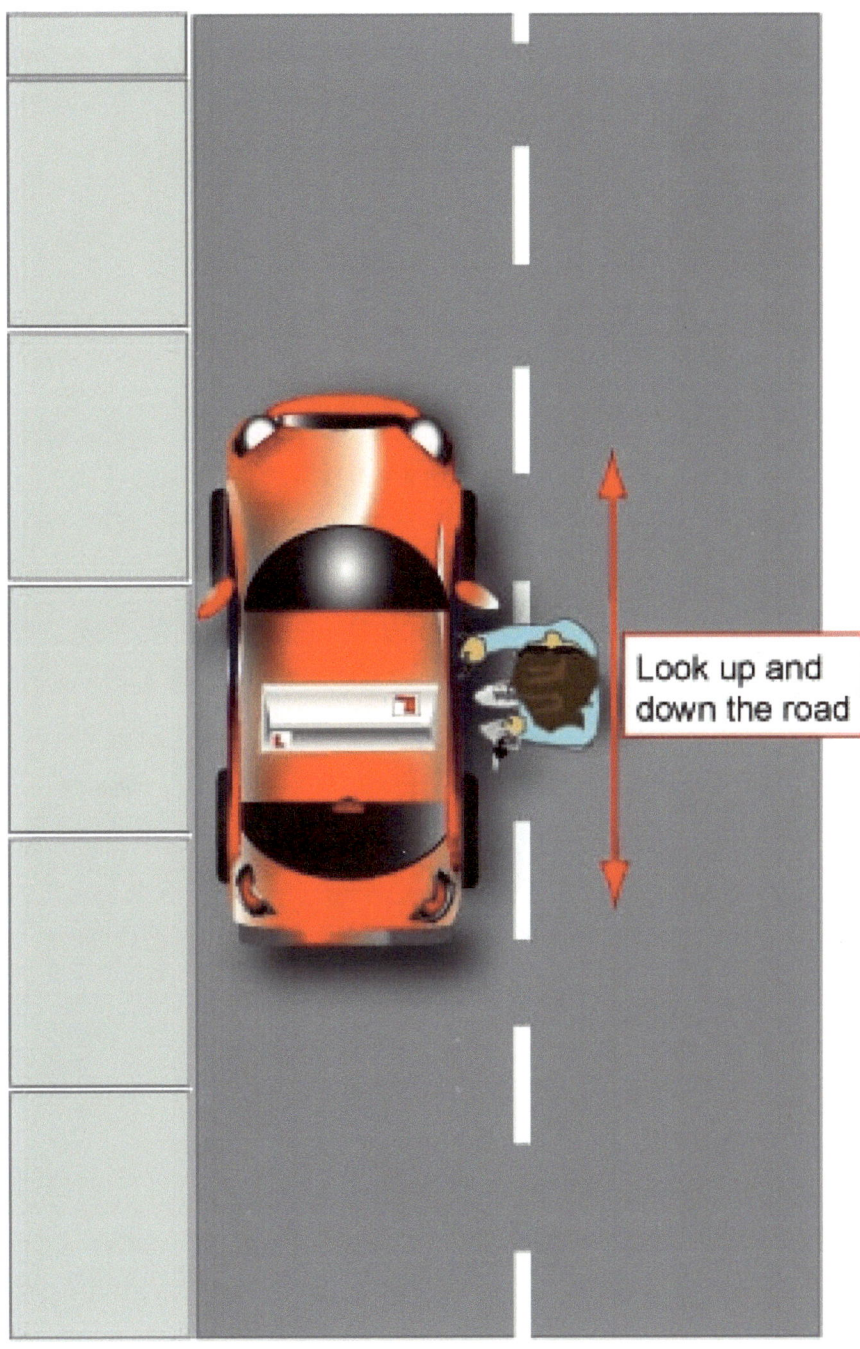

Seat

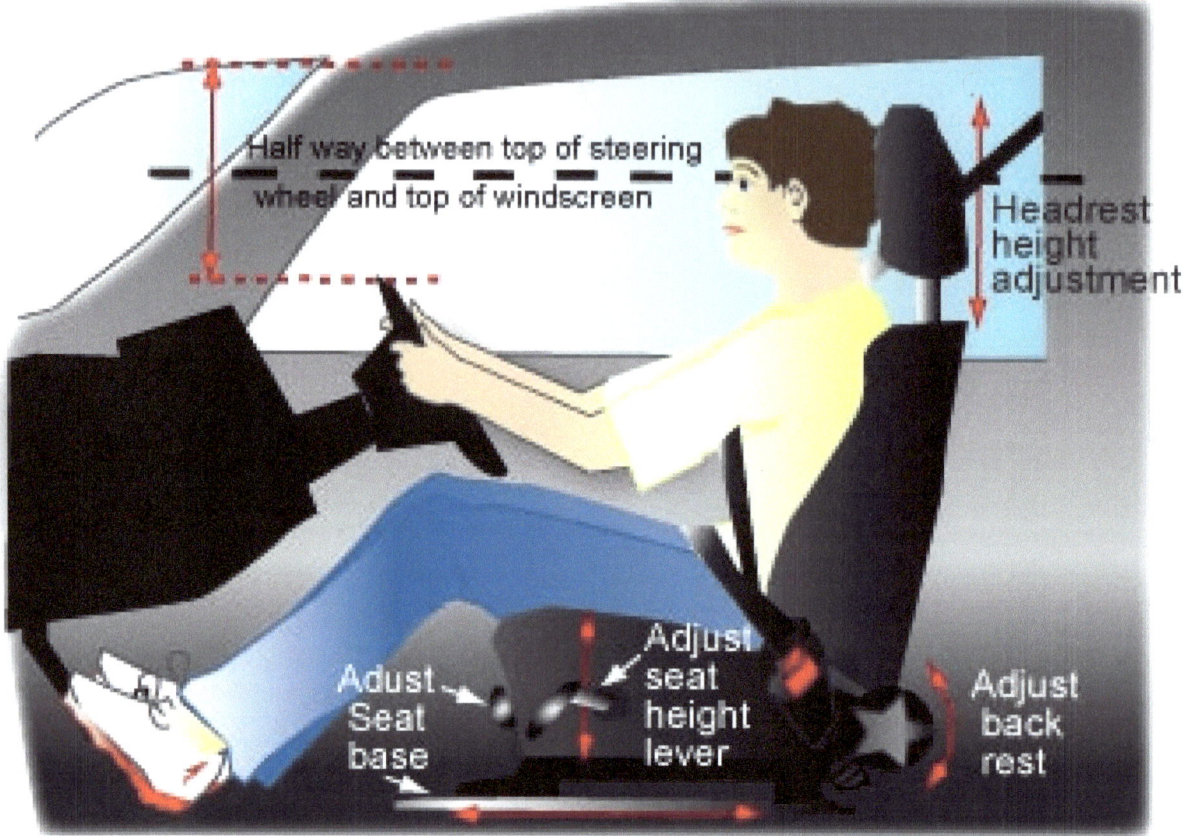

Seatbelt

Steering

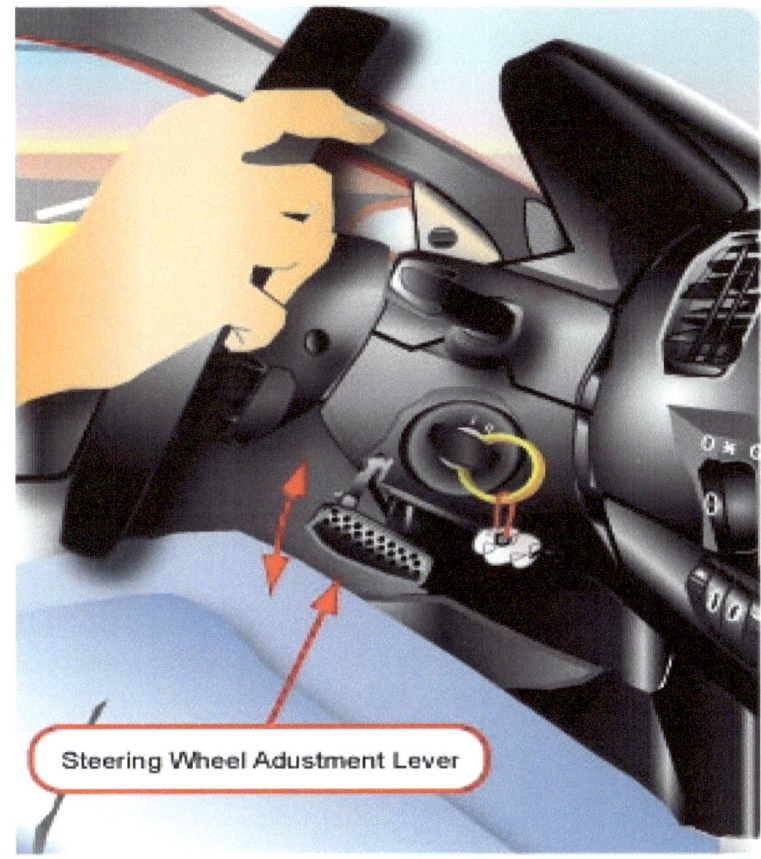

Steering Wheel Adustment Lever

Copyright Bill Bryans, Instructor Training Services, 2009

Mirrors

Mirror Zones of Vision & Blind Spots

Move Off Look

Copy right Bill Bryans, Instructor Training Services, 2009

Accelerator

Footbrake

Clutch

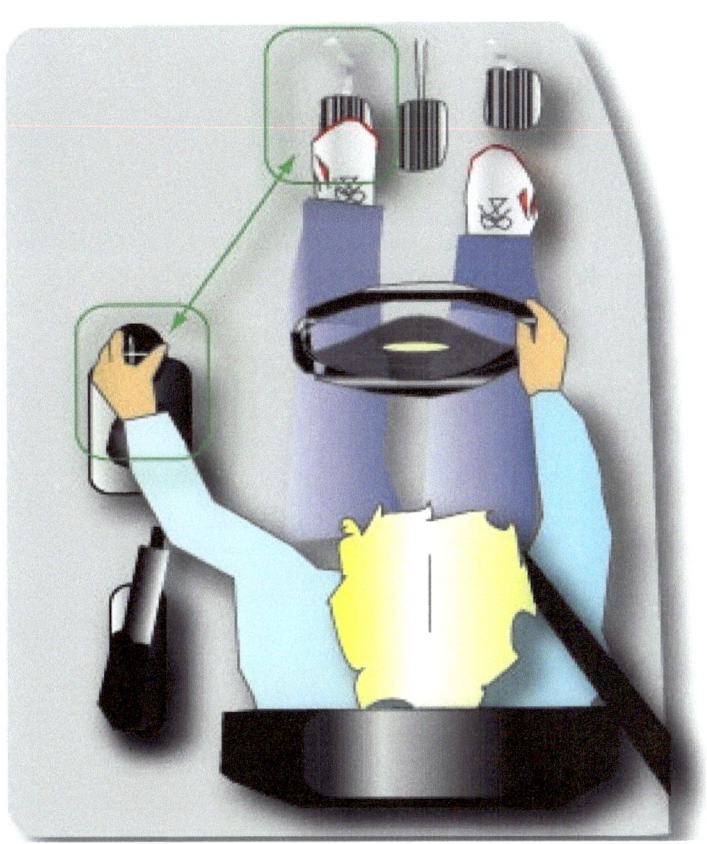

Gears

Handbrake

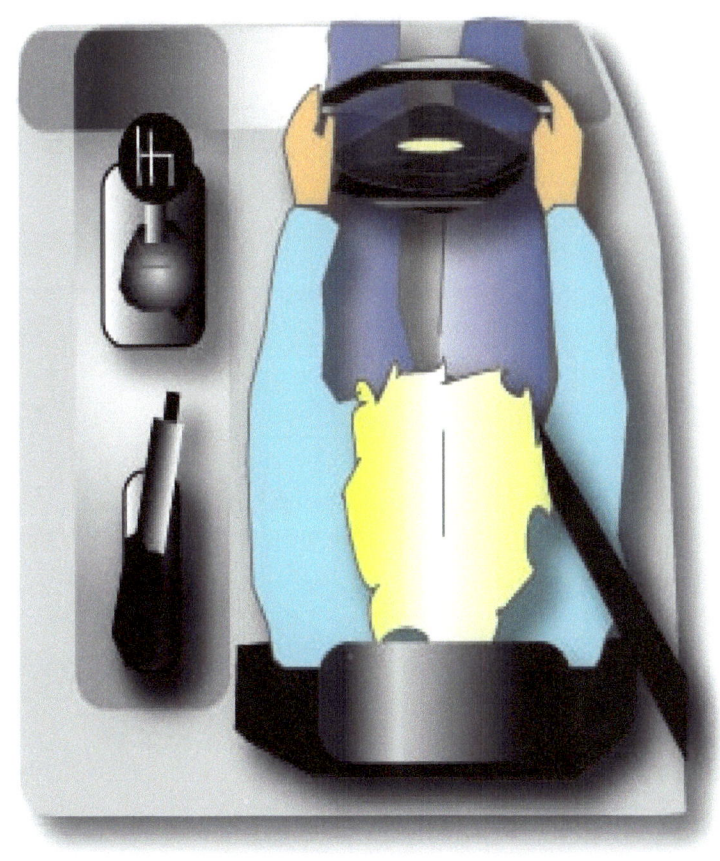

Clutch Works

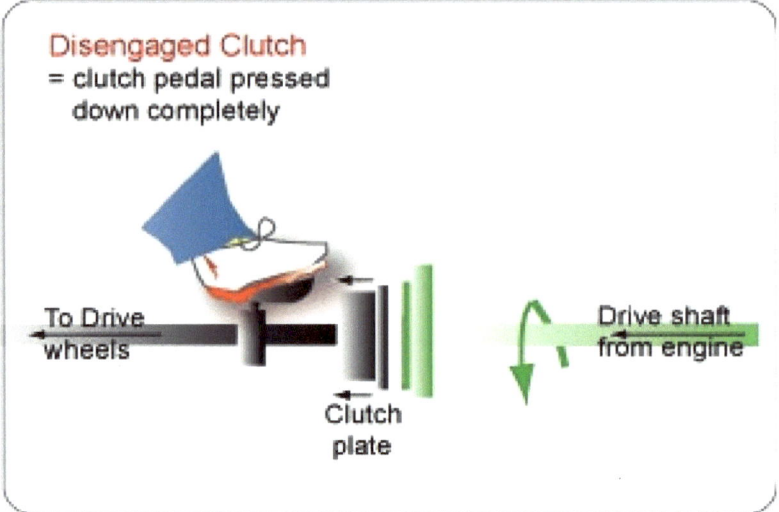

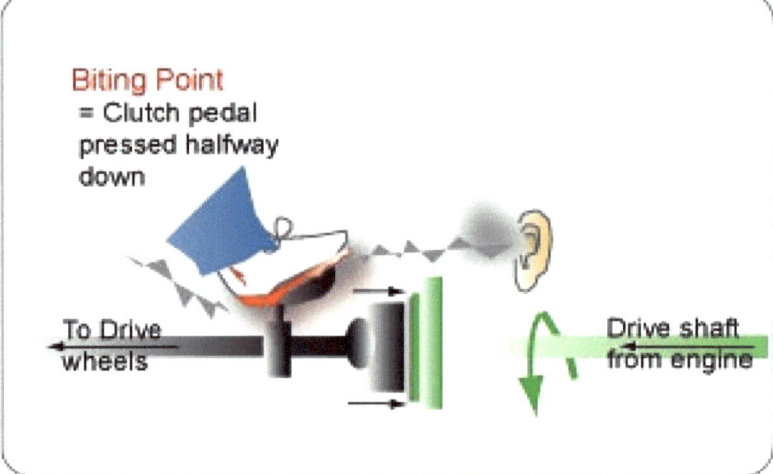

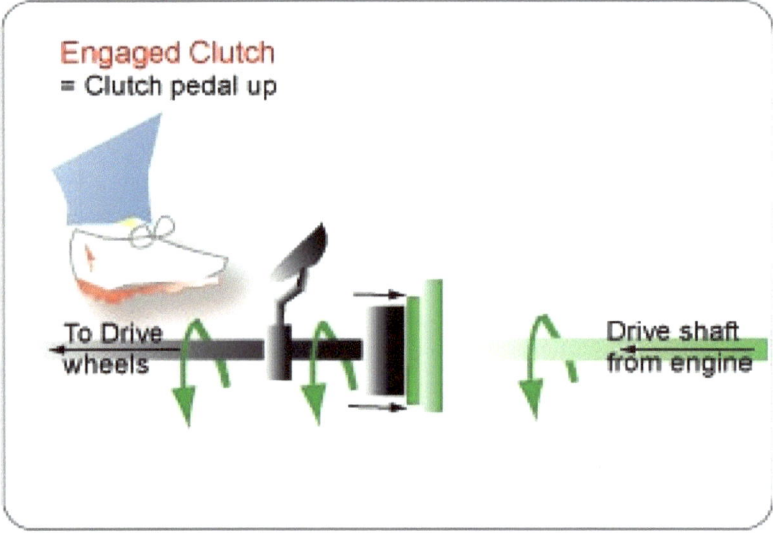

Part 2

Moving Off & Stopping

Moving Off & Stopping

Moving Off & Stopping

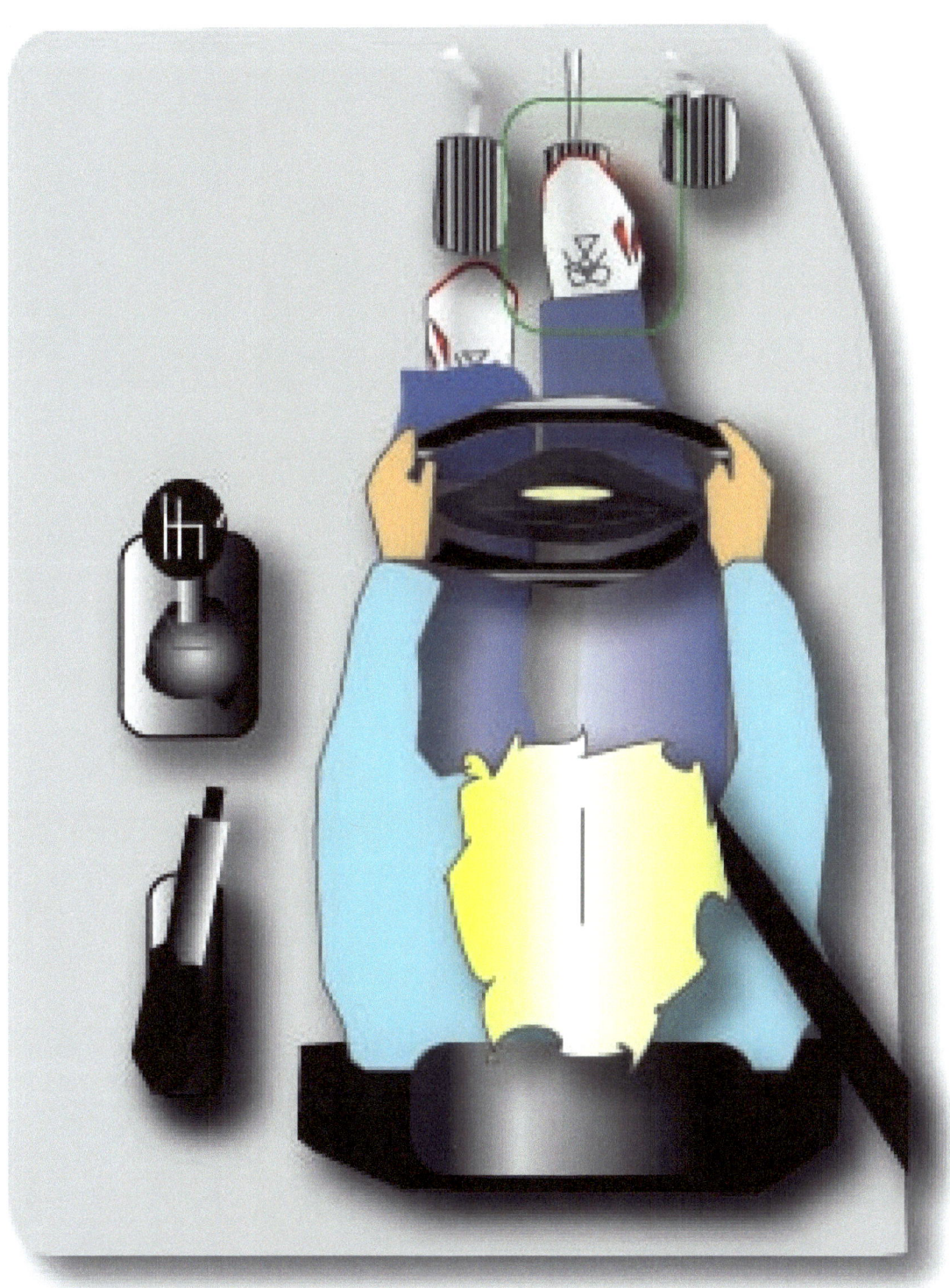

Moving Off & Stopping

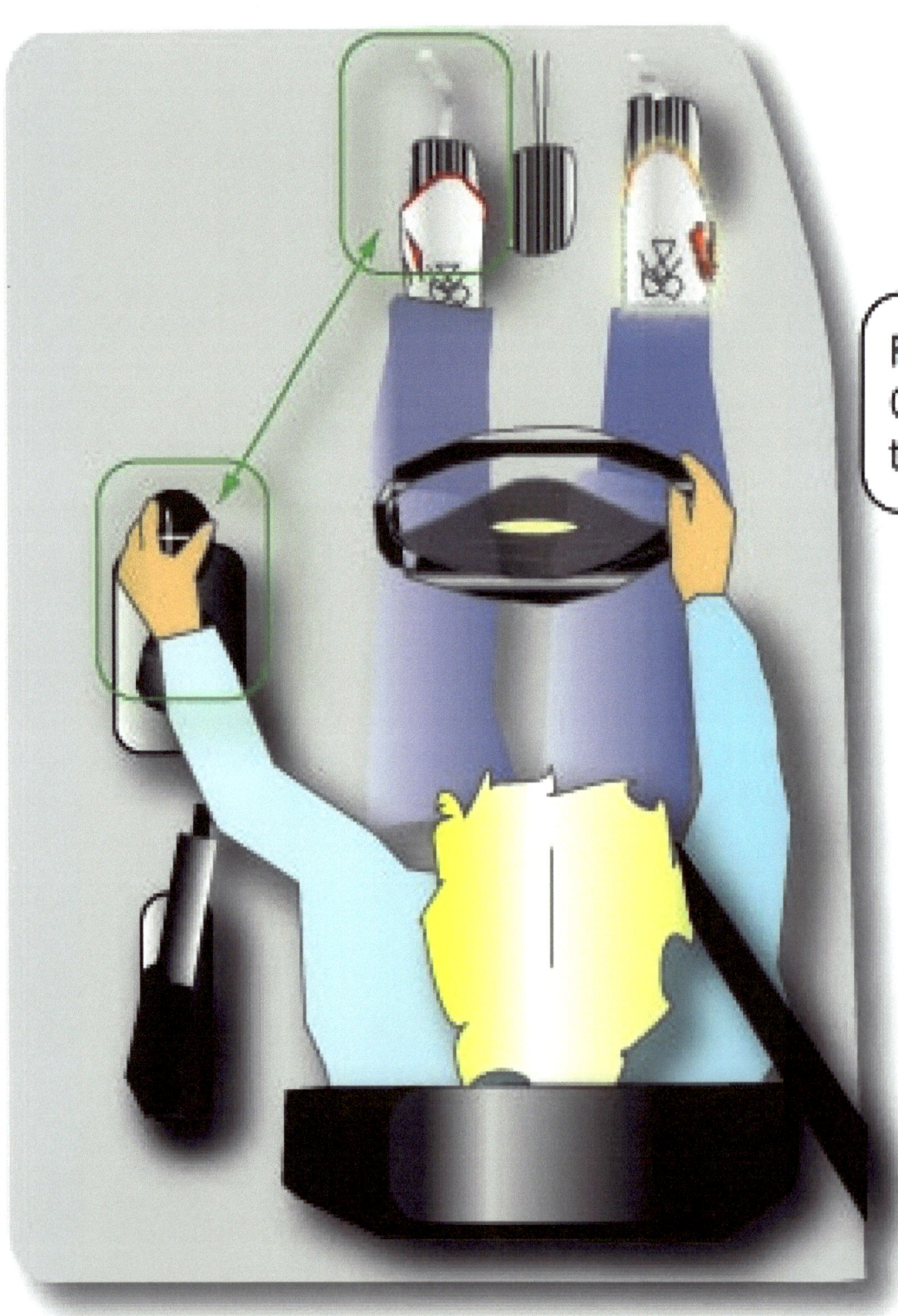

Bite Point

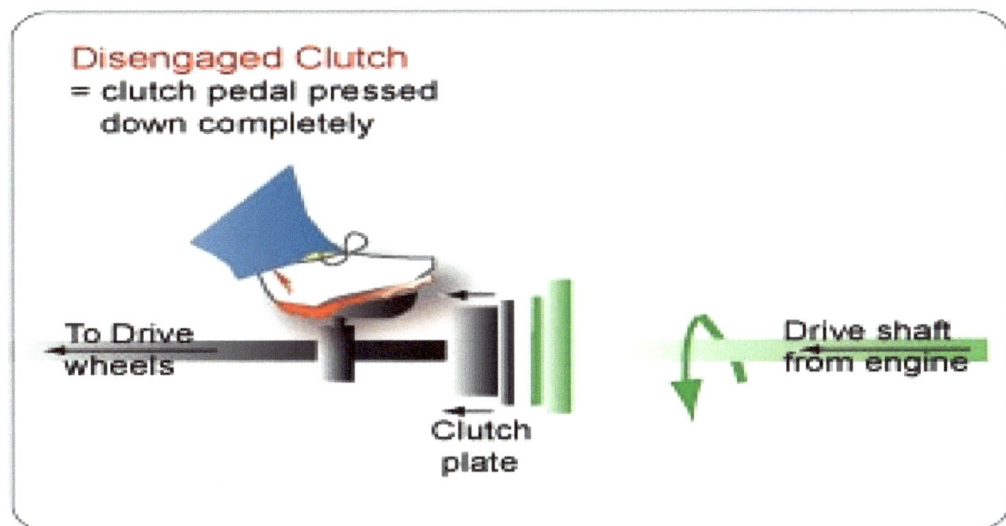

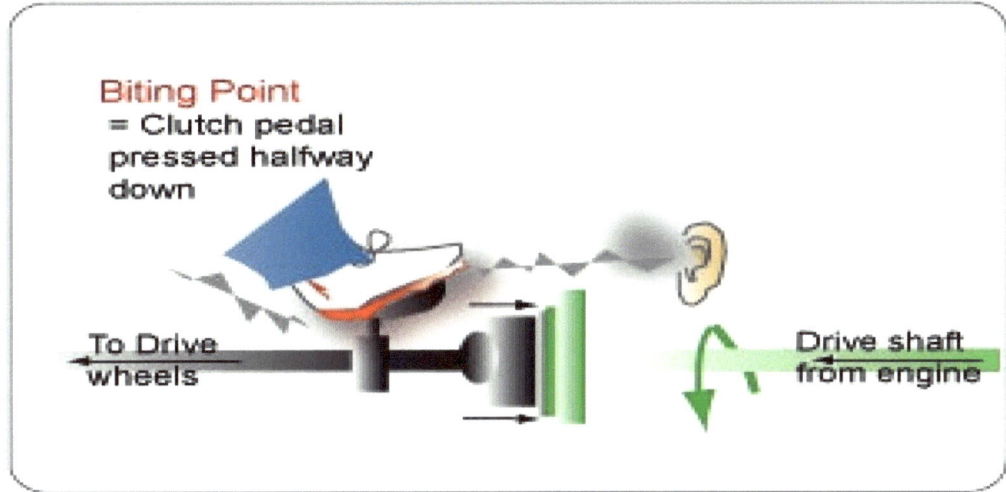

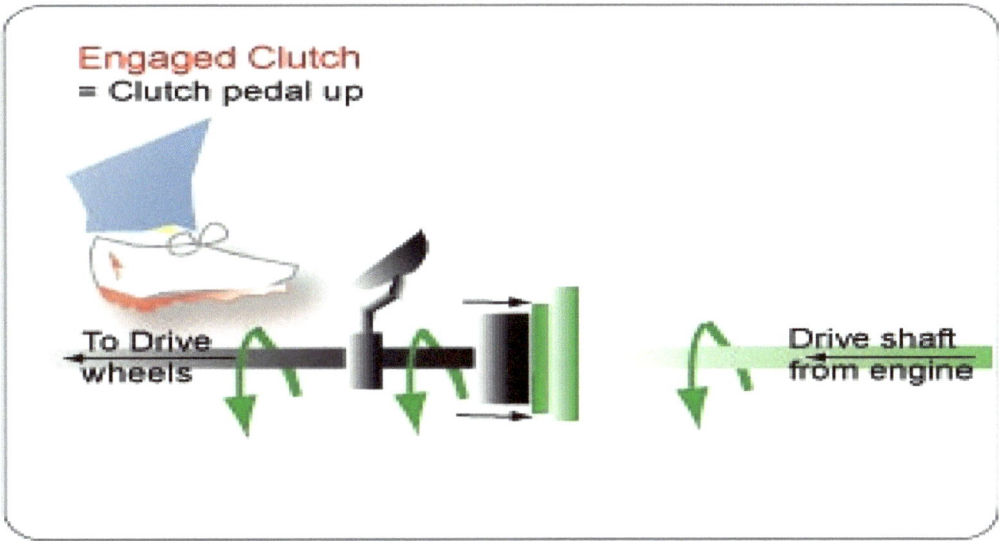

Gear & Handbrake

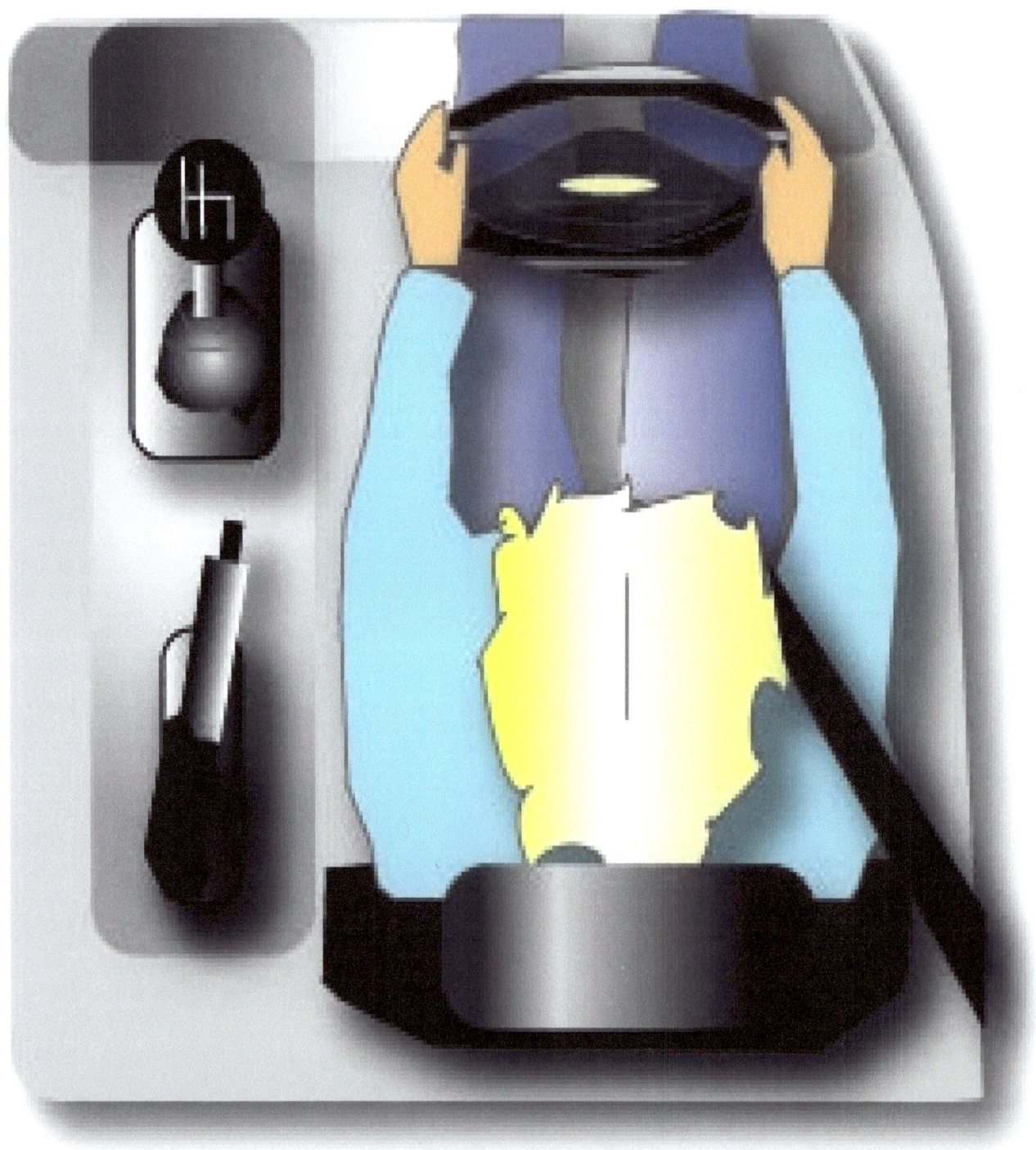

Moving Off & Stopping

Part 3

'Straight' Reversing

Straight Reversing

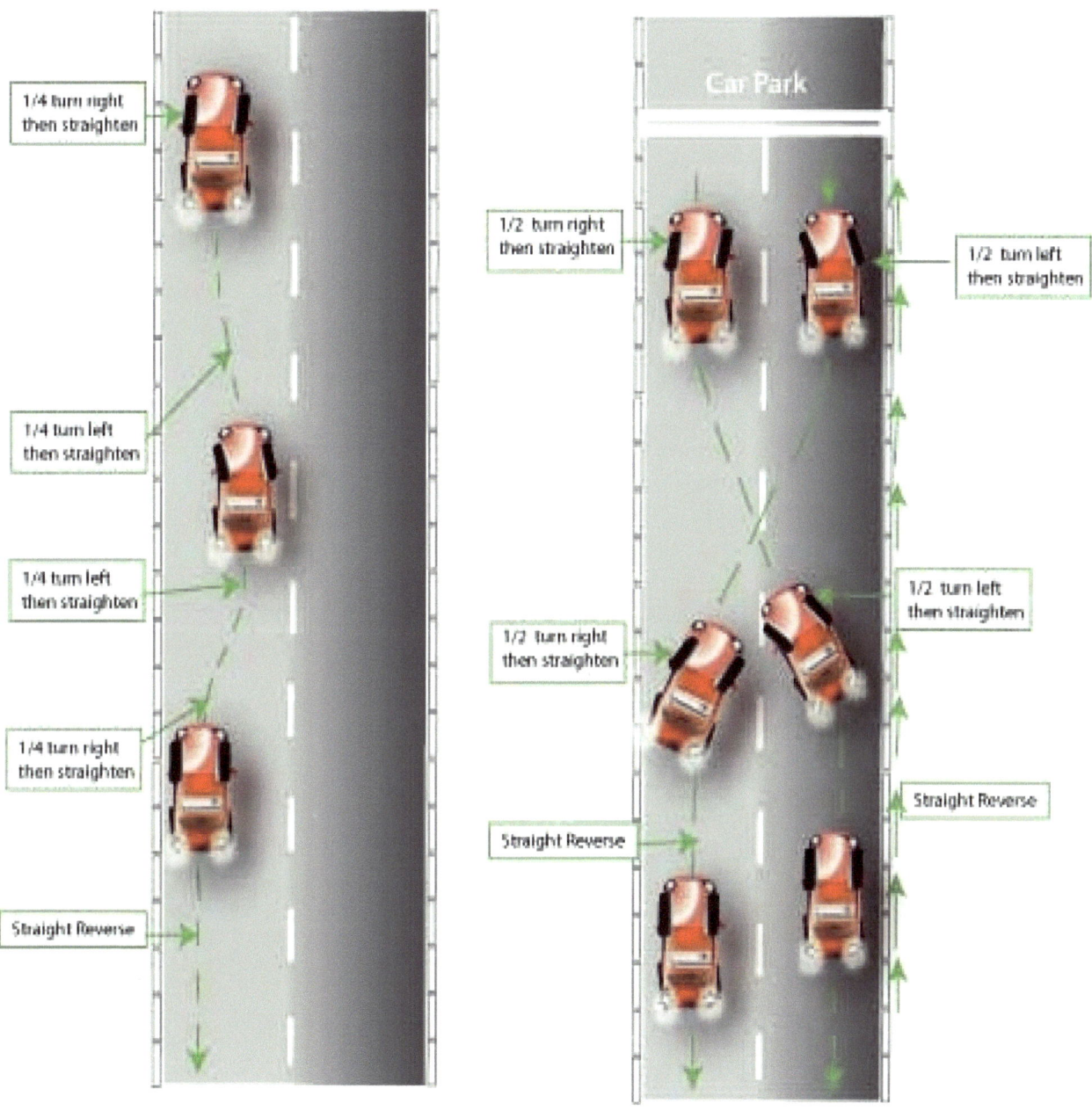

Part 4

Turn in the Road

Exercise

Turn in the Road – Control - Accuracy

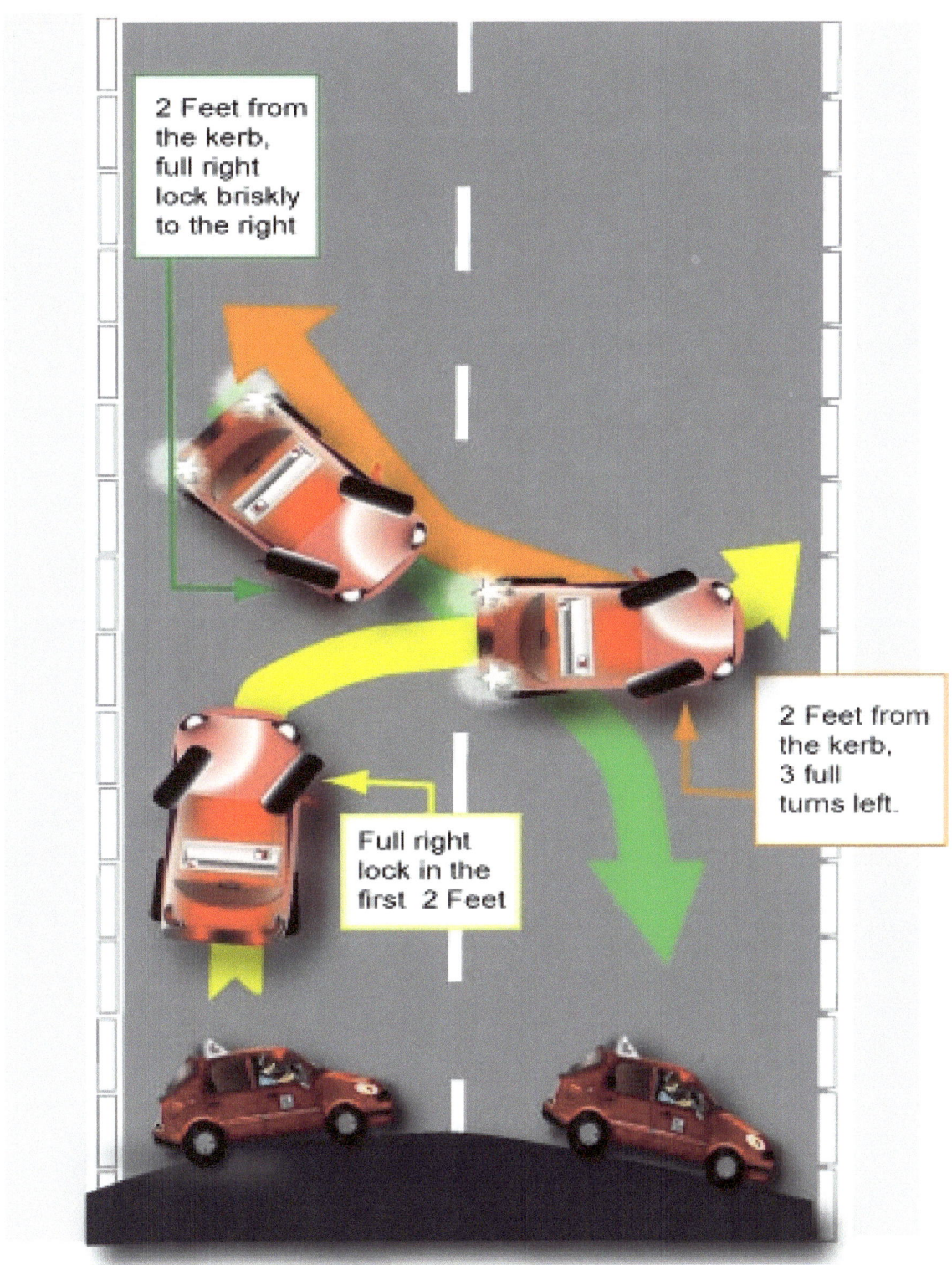

Turn in the Road - Observation

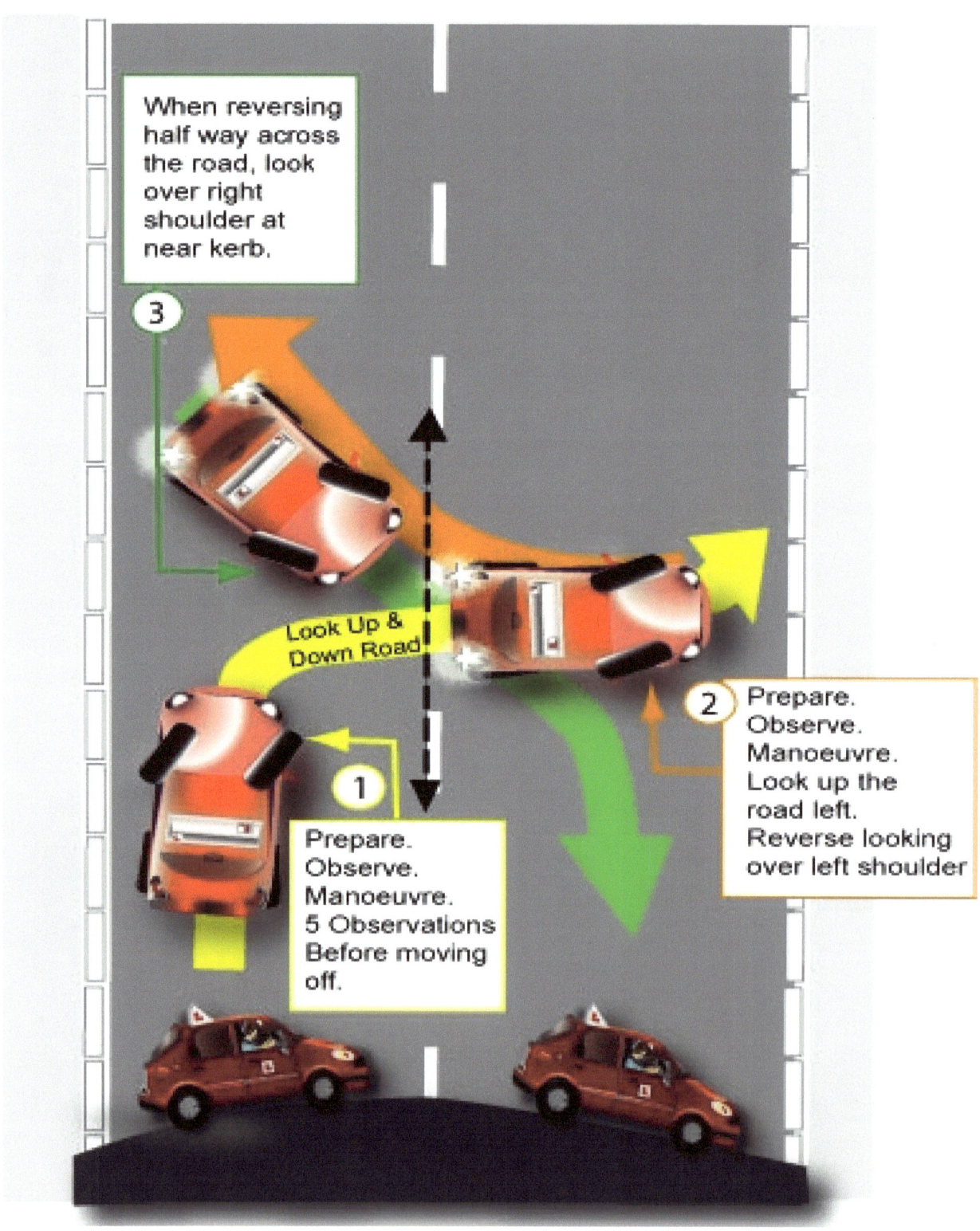

Part 5

Reverse to the Left

Reversing to the Left – Control - Accuracy

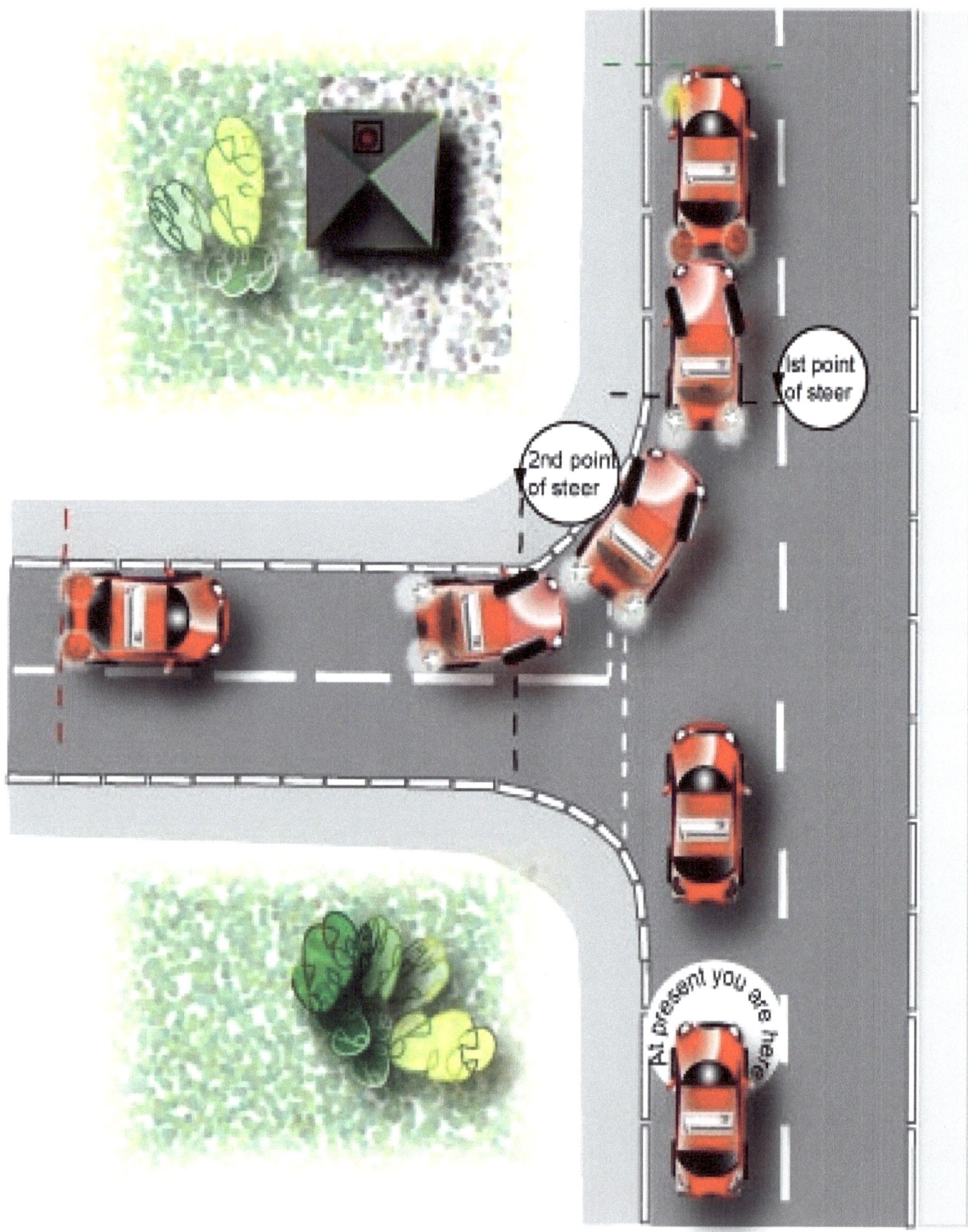

Reversing to the Left - Observation

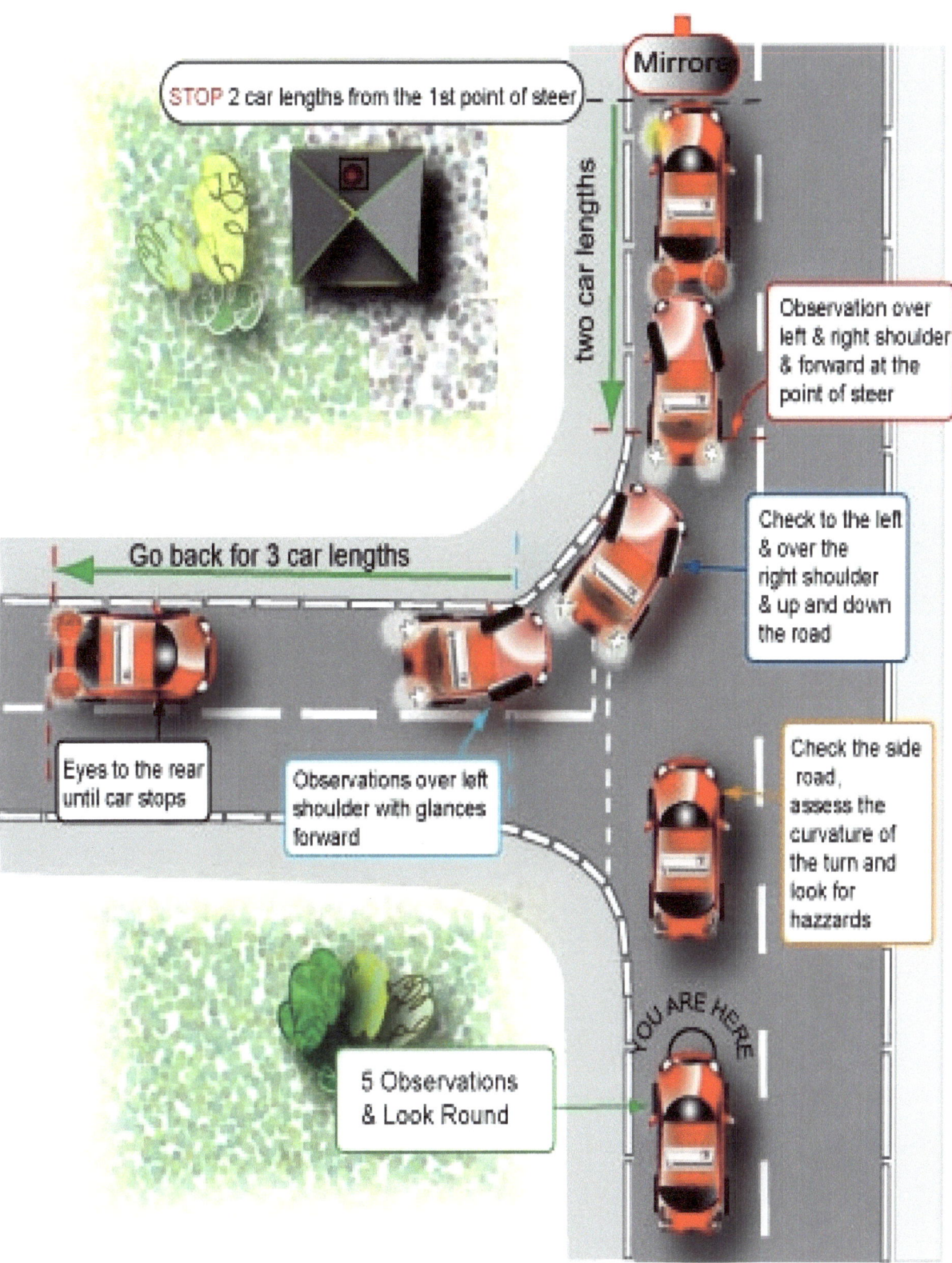

Part 6

Reverse to the Right

Reversing to the Right – Control - Accuracy

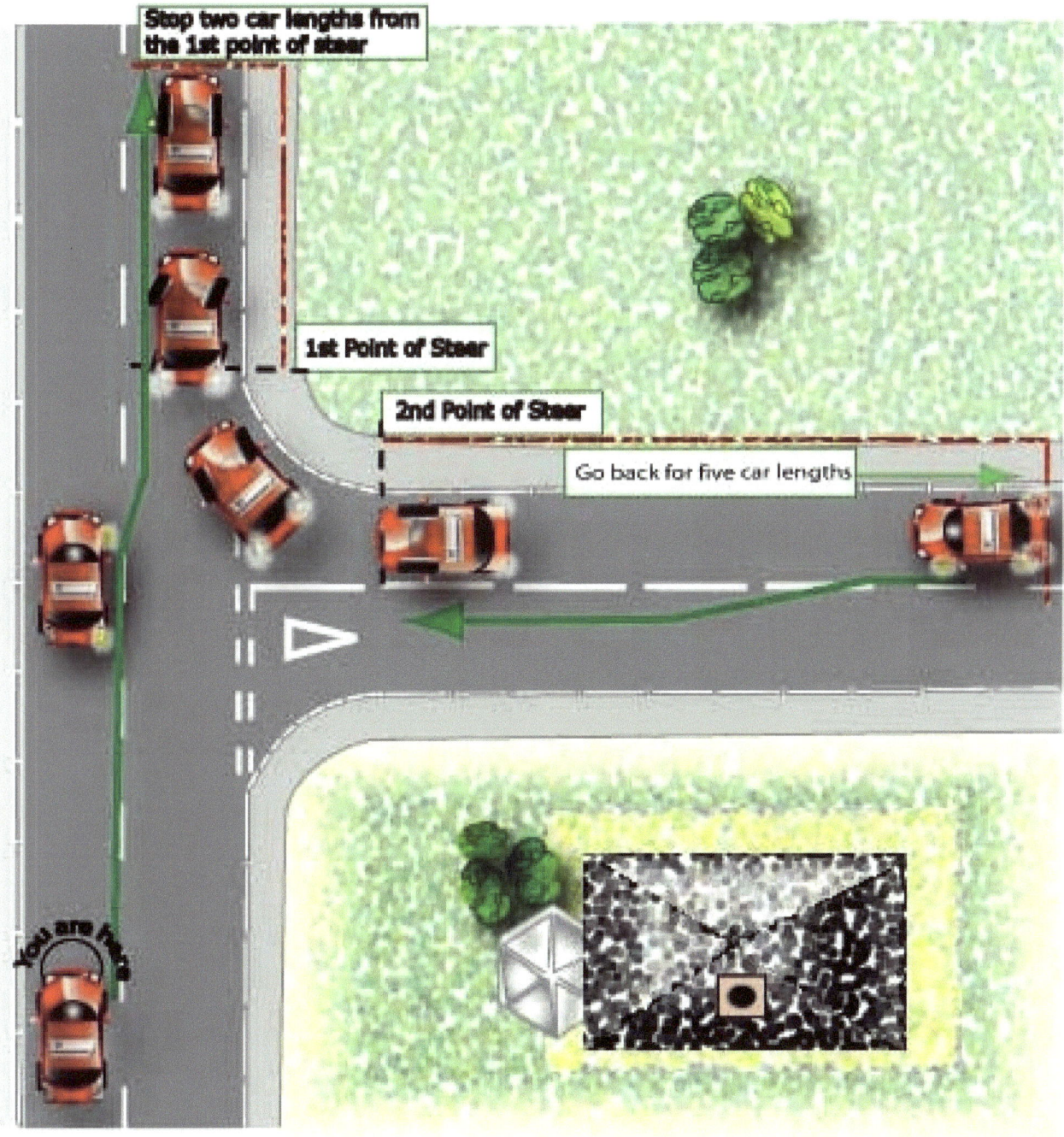

Reversing to the Right - Observation

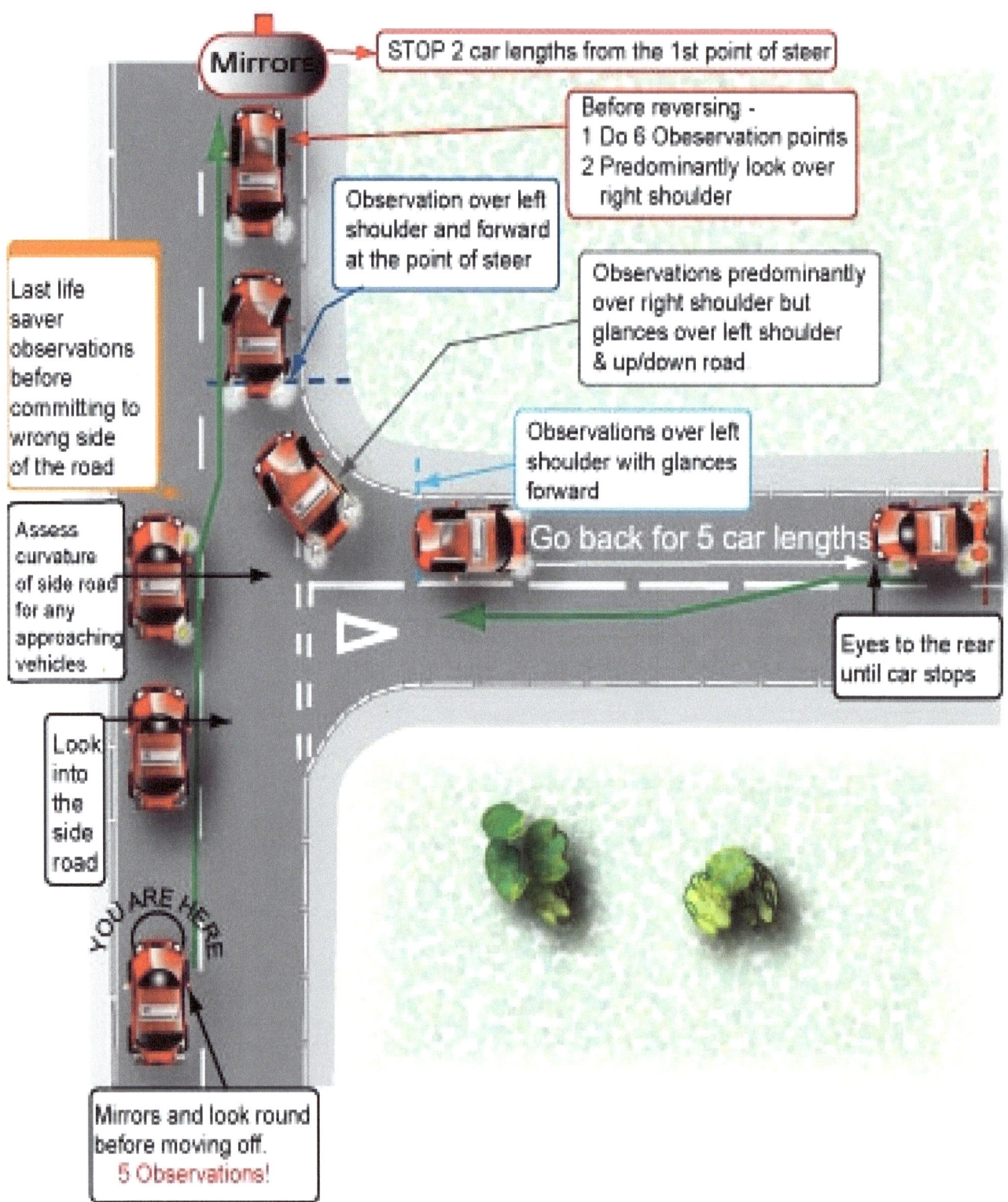

Part 7

Simulated Pupil

Examination

Reverse Park

Reverse Park – Control - Accuracy

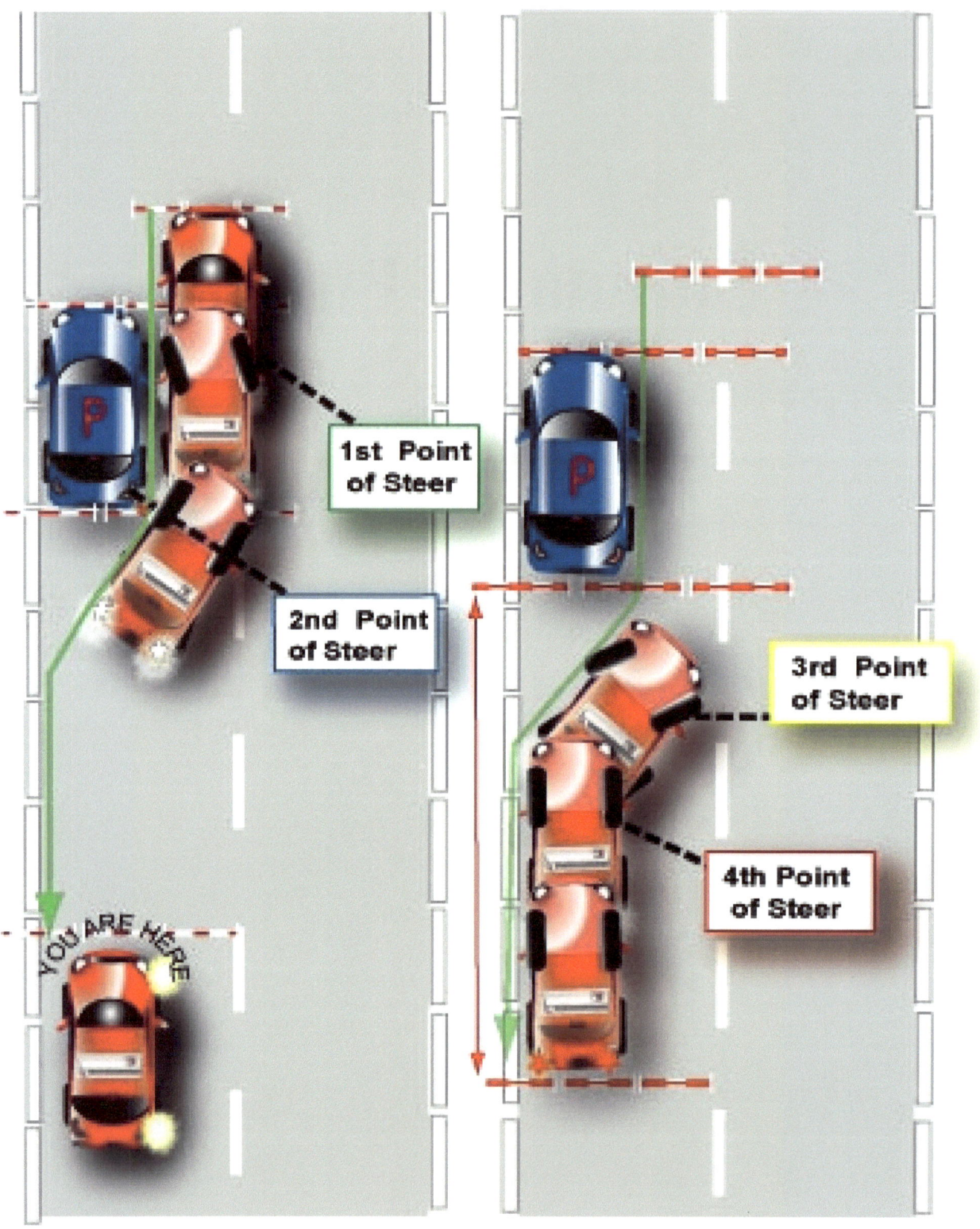

Reverse Park – Observation

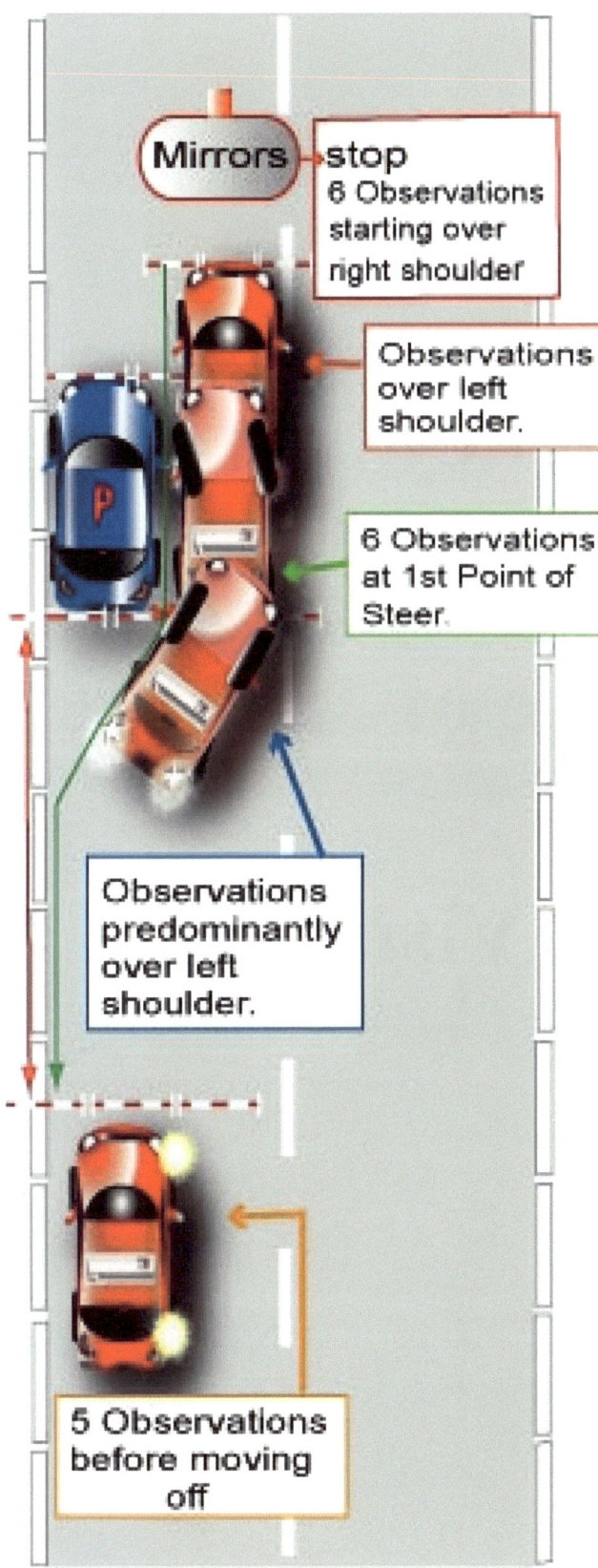
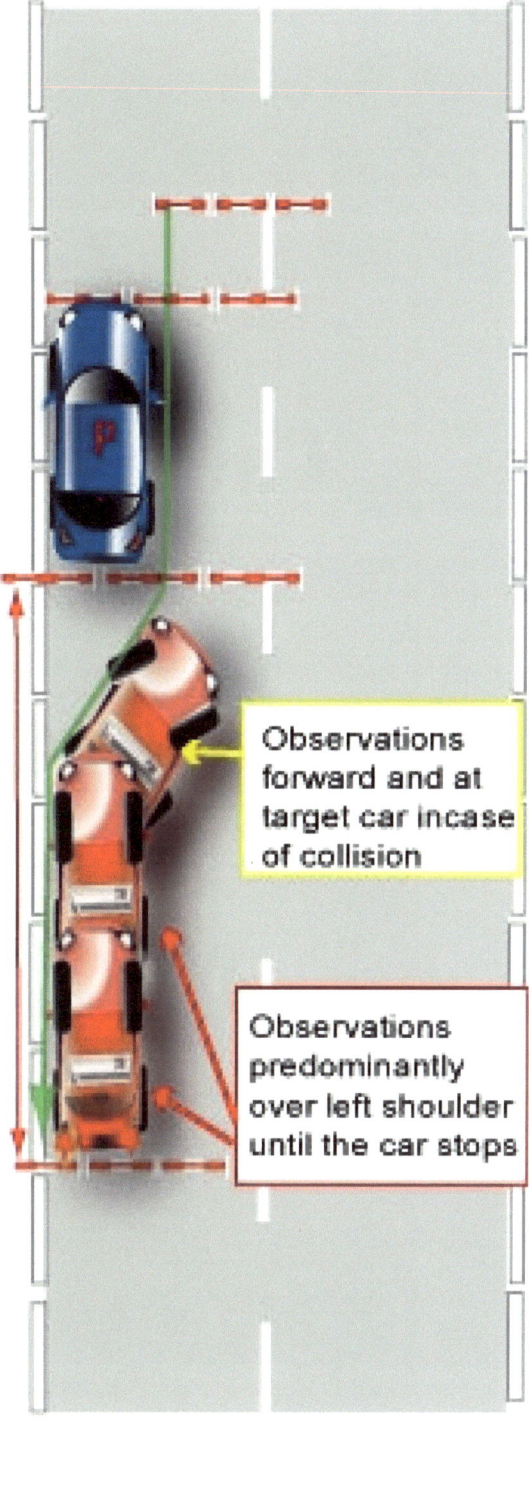

Copyright Bill Bryans, Instructor Training Services, 2009

Part 8

The Emergency Stop

The Correct Use of Mirrors

& Mirror Vision

Mirrors

Copyright Bill Bryans, Instructor Training Services, 2009

Mirrors

Mirror Zones of Vision & Blind Spots

Move Off Look

Copy right Bill Bryans, Instruc

Mirrors: Quick Sideways Glance

Mirror Vision

Act correctly on what you see!

Mirrors

MS-PSGL

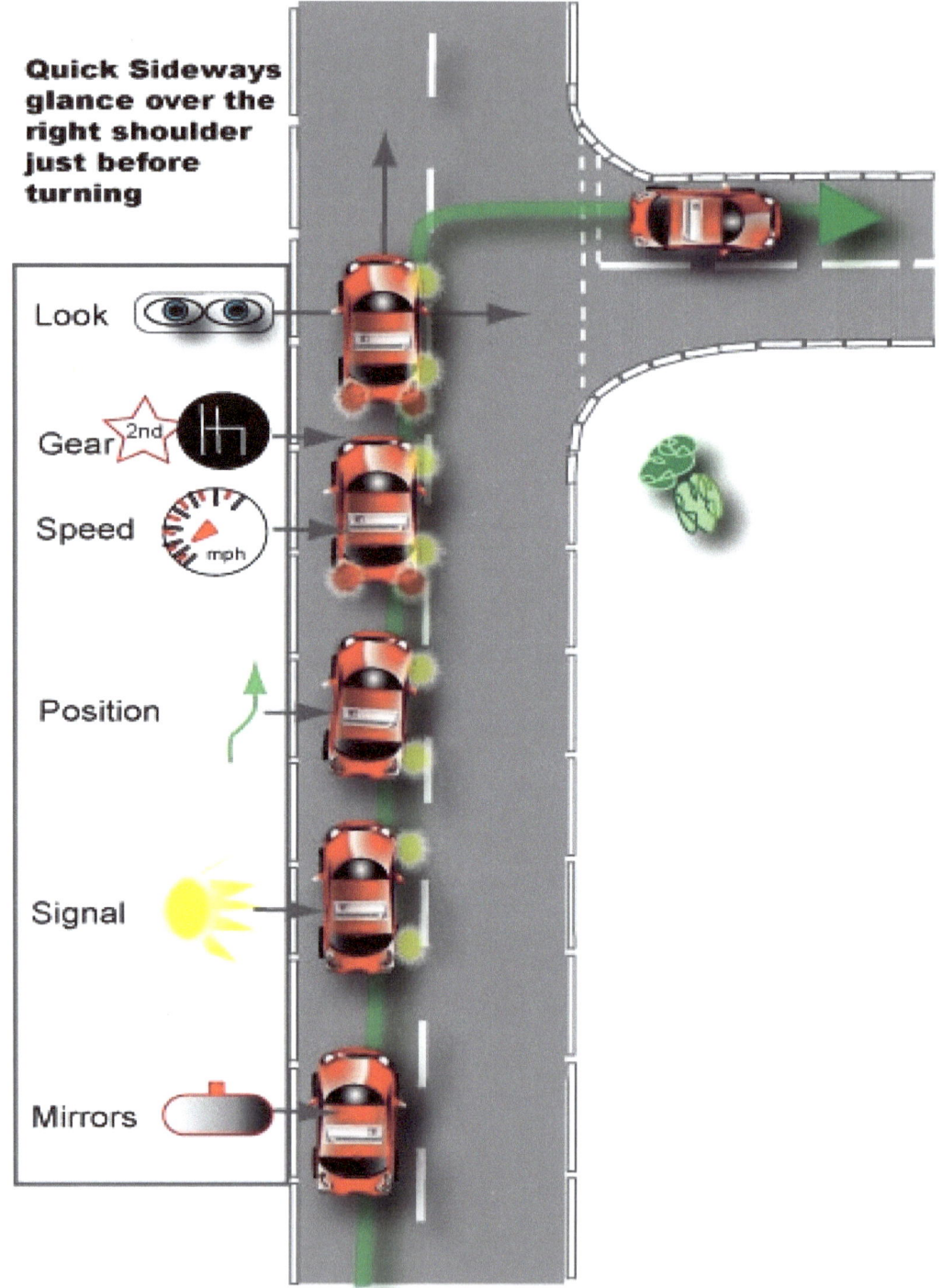

Emergency Stop
Check Behind

The Audio – Visual Signal

Emergency Stop – Foot Brake & Clutch

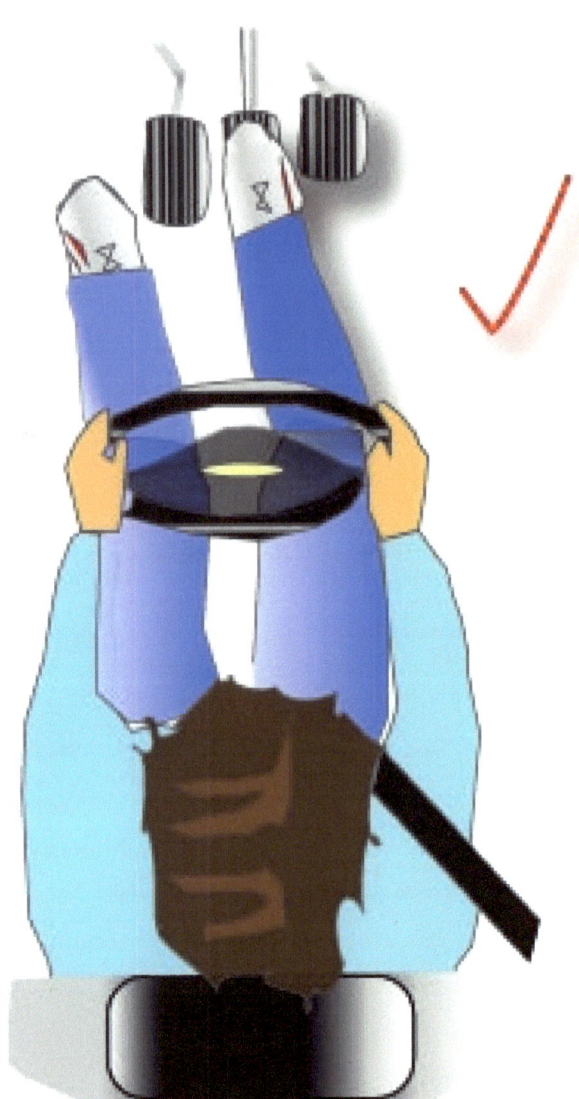 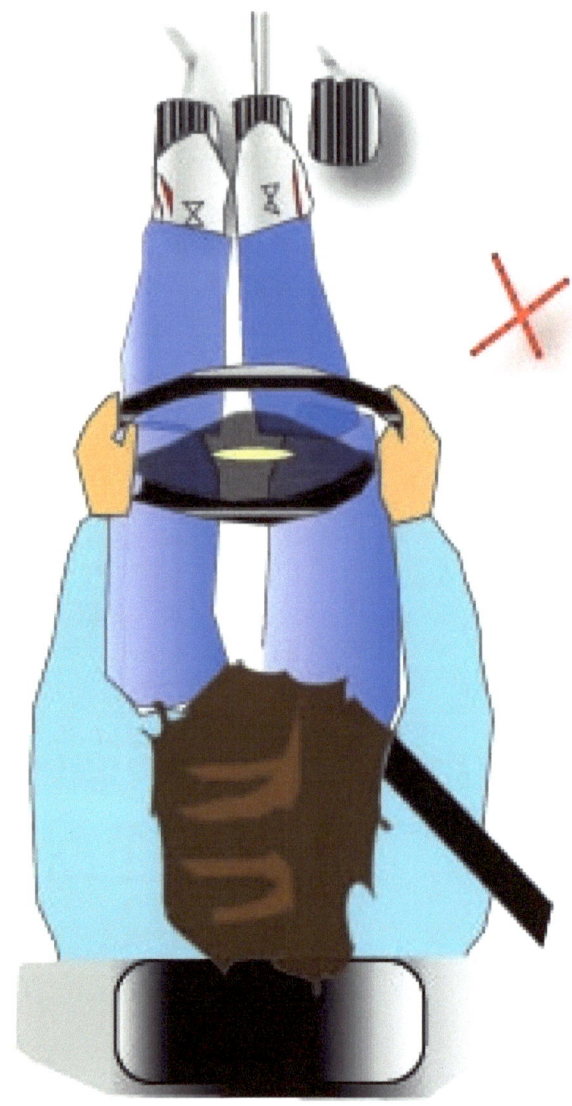

Emergency Stop - Use of the Footbrake

Emergency Stop - Aquaplaning

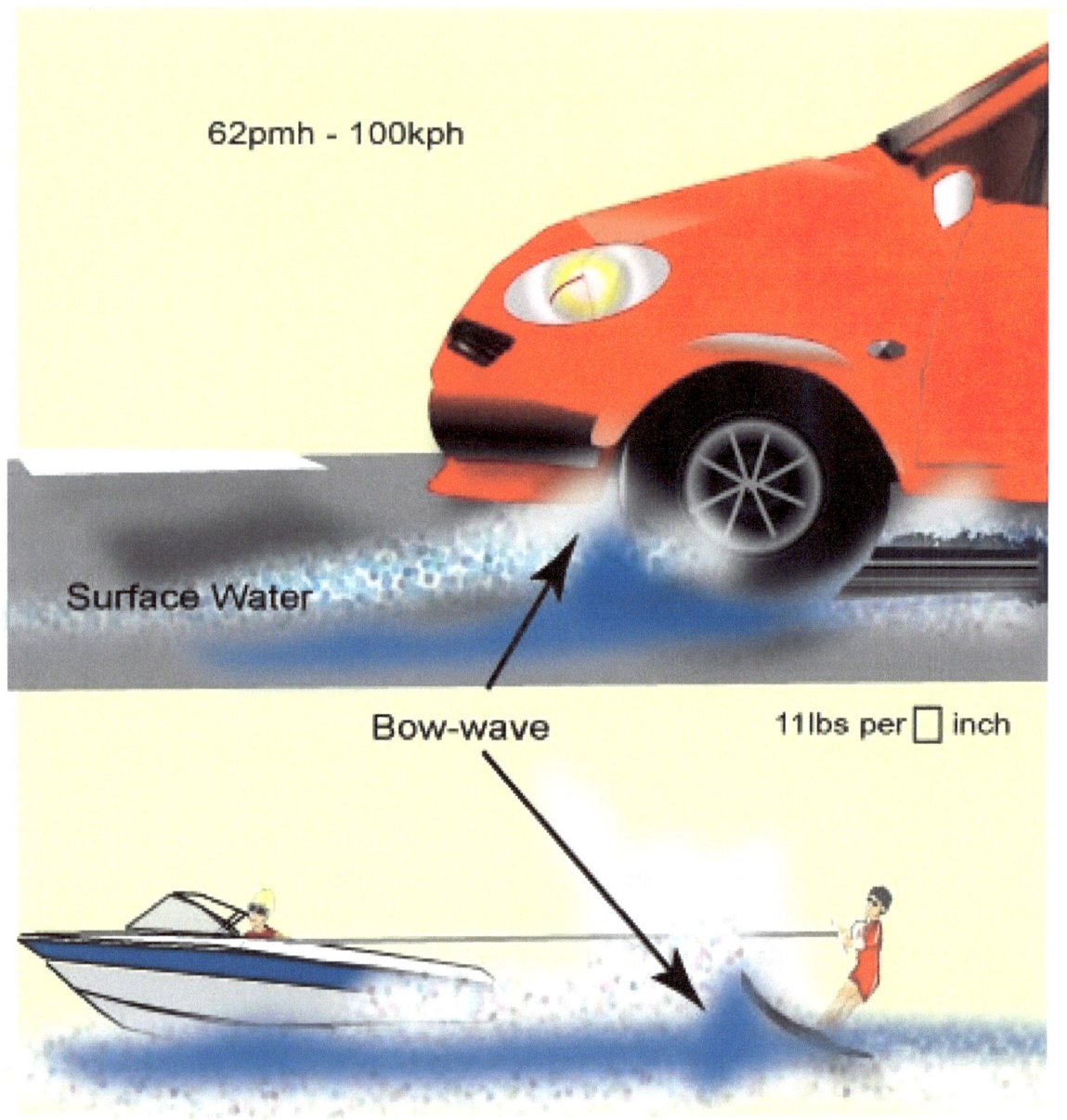

Recognition – Aquaplaning
1. Light surface water
2. Light steering
3. 62mph

Emergency Stop - Rear Wheel Skid

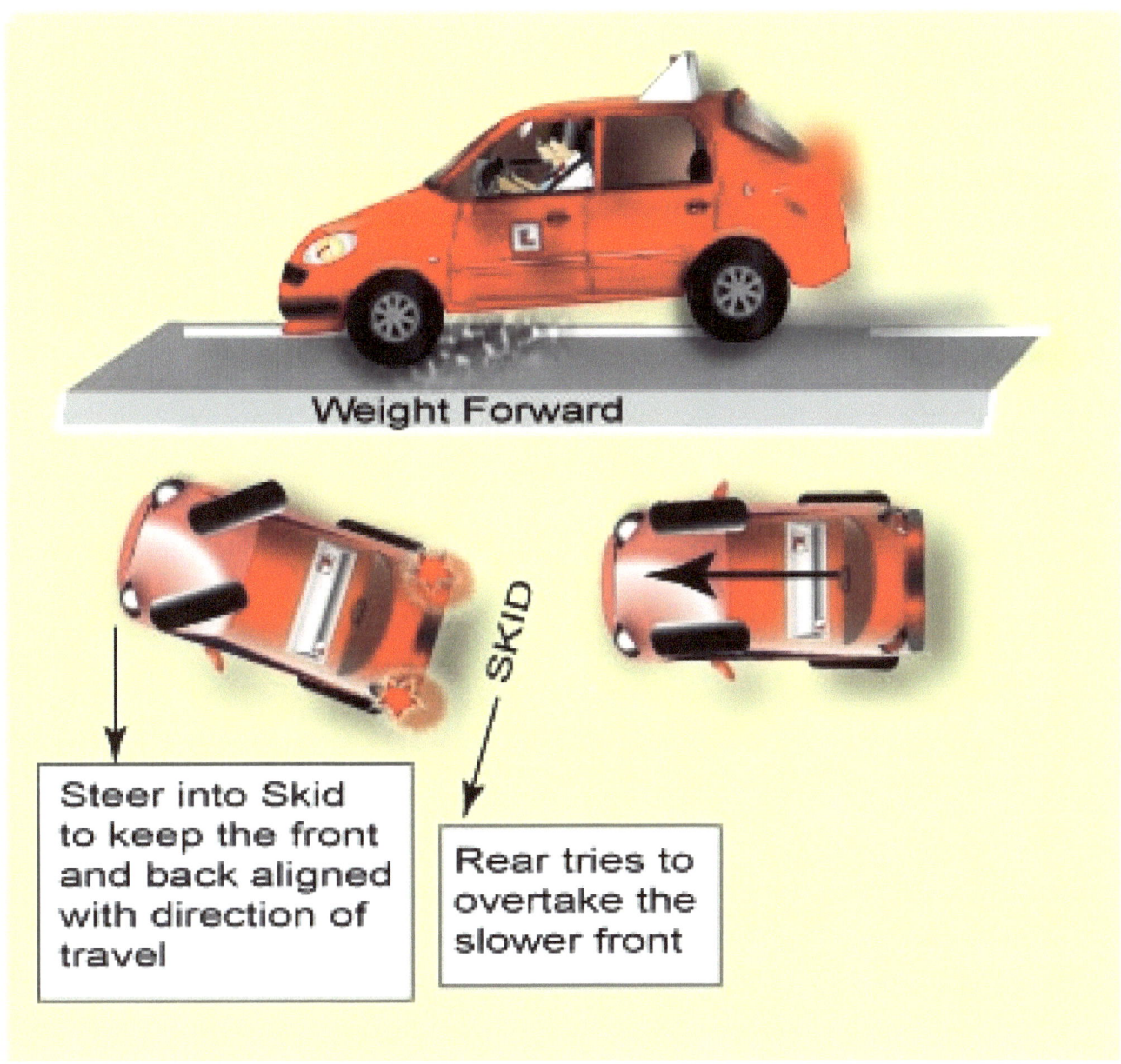

Recognition – The Rear Wheel Skid
1. A Slither rather than a screech
2. A Skid to the left or right
3. A skid to the left is more likely due to the camber of the road

Emergency Stop - Front Wheel Skid

Recognition - The Three 'S's
1. Smoke
2. Screech
3. Smell

Part 9

Junctions Major to Minor

Junctions Major to Minor

Recognition of the Hazard

Road Signs (100 meters)

    Signs Directional

    Yellow Box Junctions

    'Keep Clear' Written on the Road

    Traffic Light Sequence

White Lines

    'Give Way Lines' or 'Priority Lines'

    Hazard Warning Lines in the Side Road

    Hazard Warning Lines on the Priority Route

Gaps in;

    Walls

    Hedges

    Buildings

Buildings

    Different Shaped Buildings

    Different Heights of Buildings

    Different Roof Lines

    Gabble Ends of Buildings

Junctions when Turning Left from Major to Minor

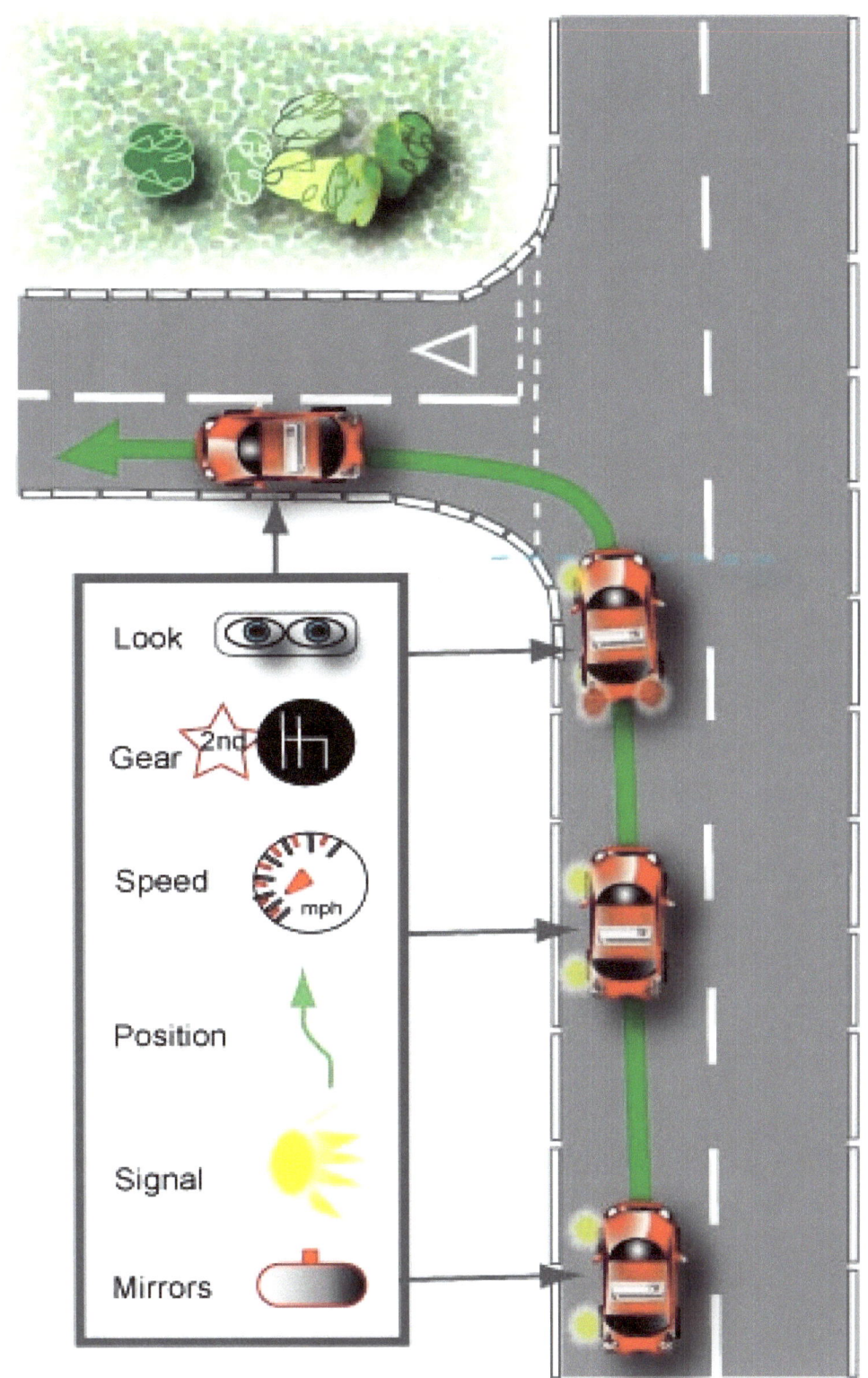

Junctions when Turning Right from Major to Minor

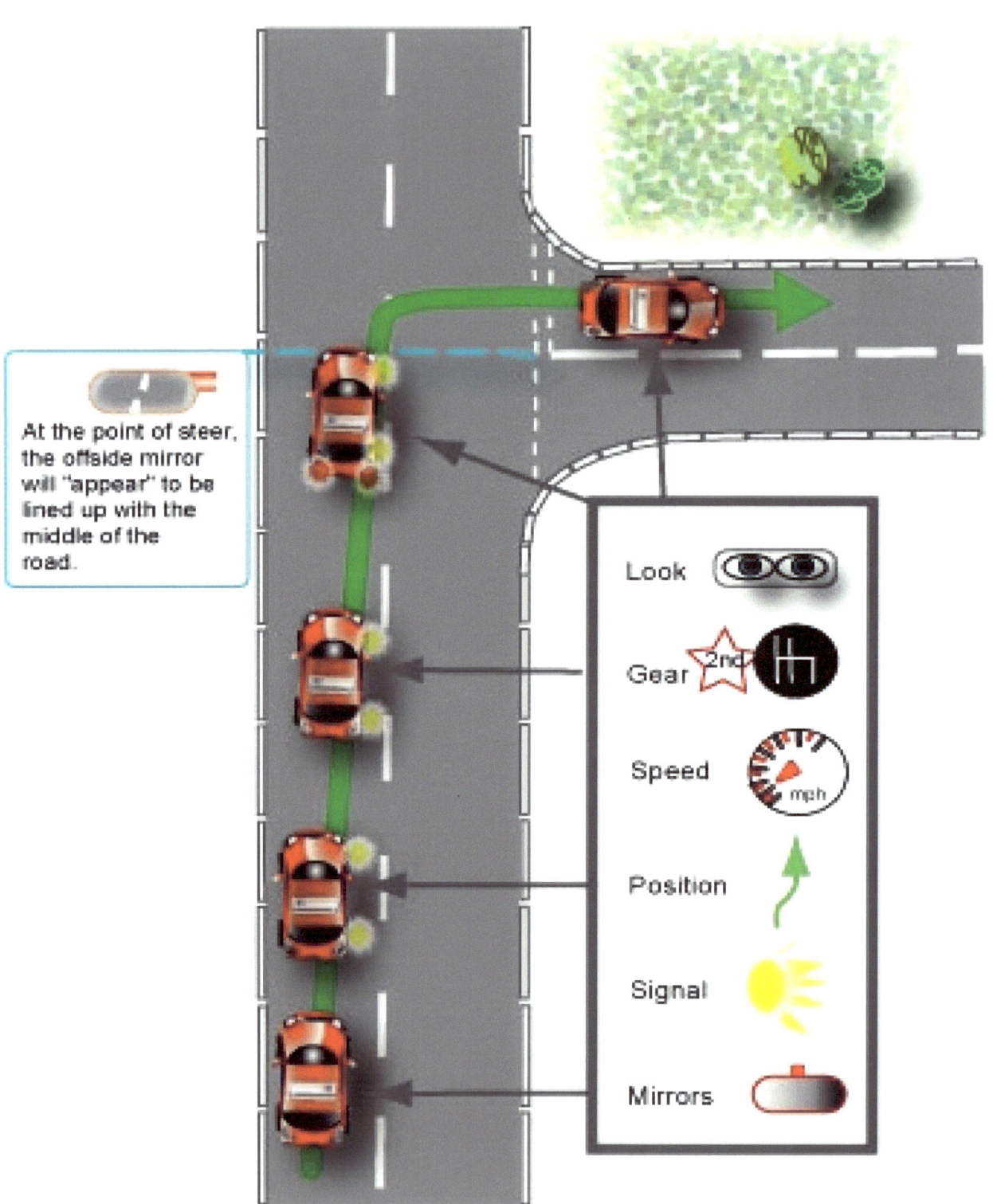

Junctions when Turning Right – Dual Carriageways

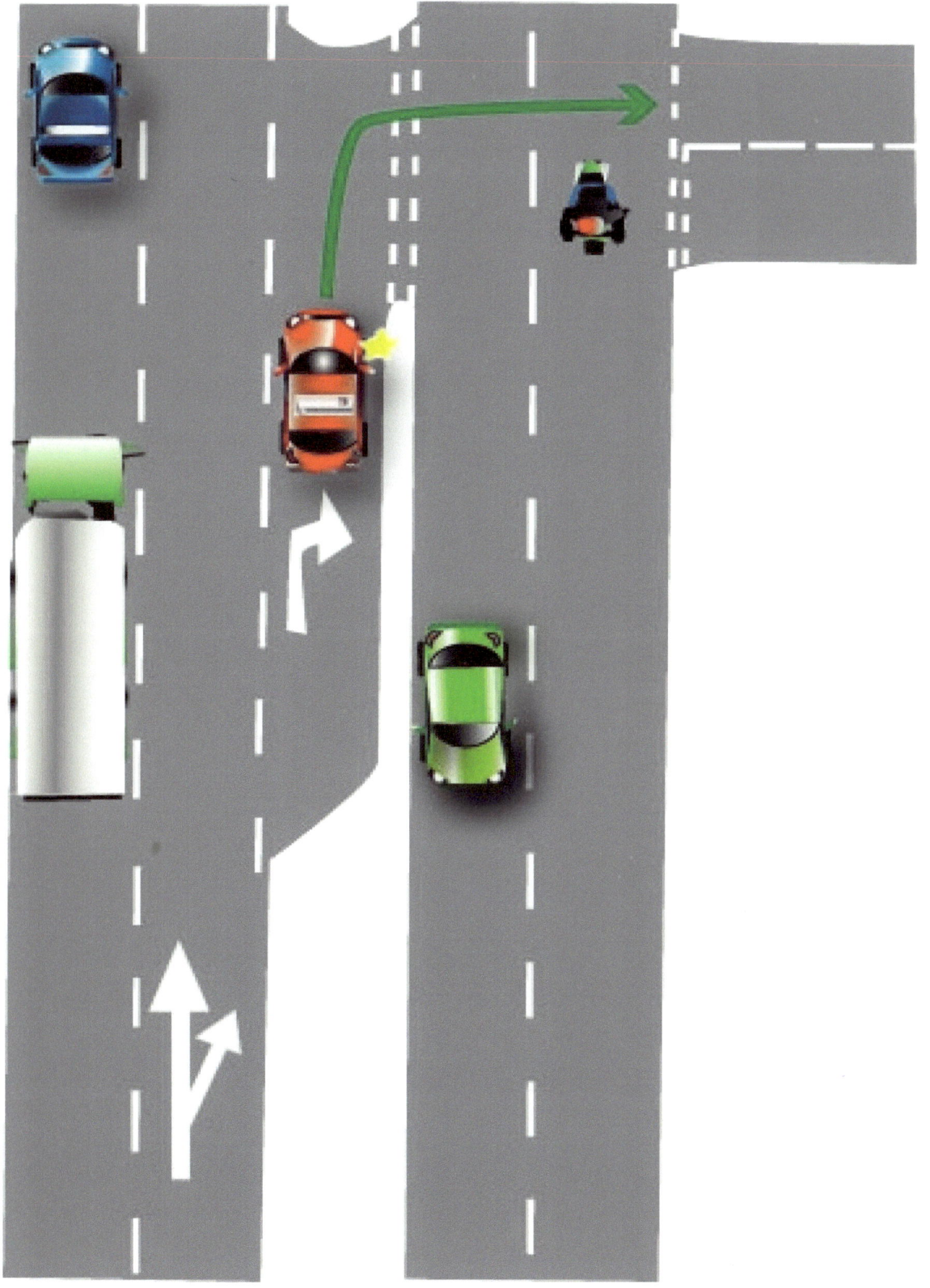

Junctions Turning right Major to Minor Cutting Across Approaching Traffic

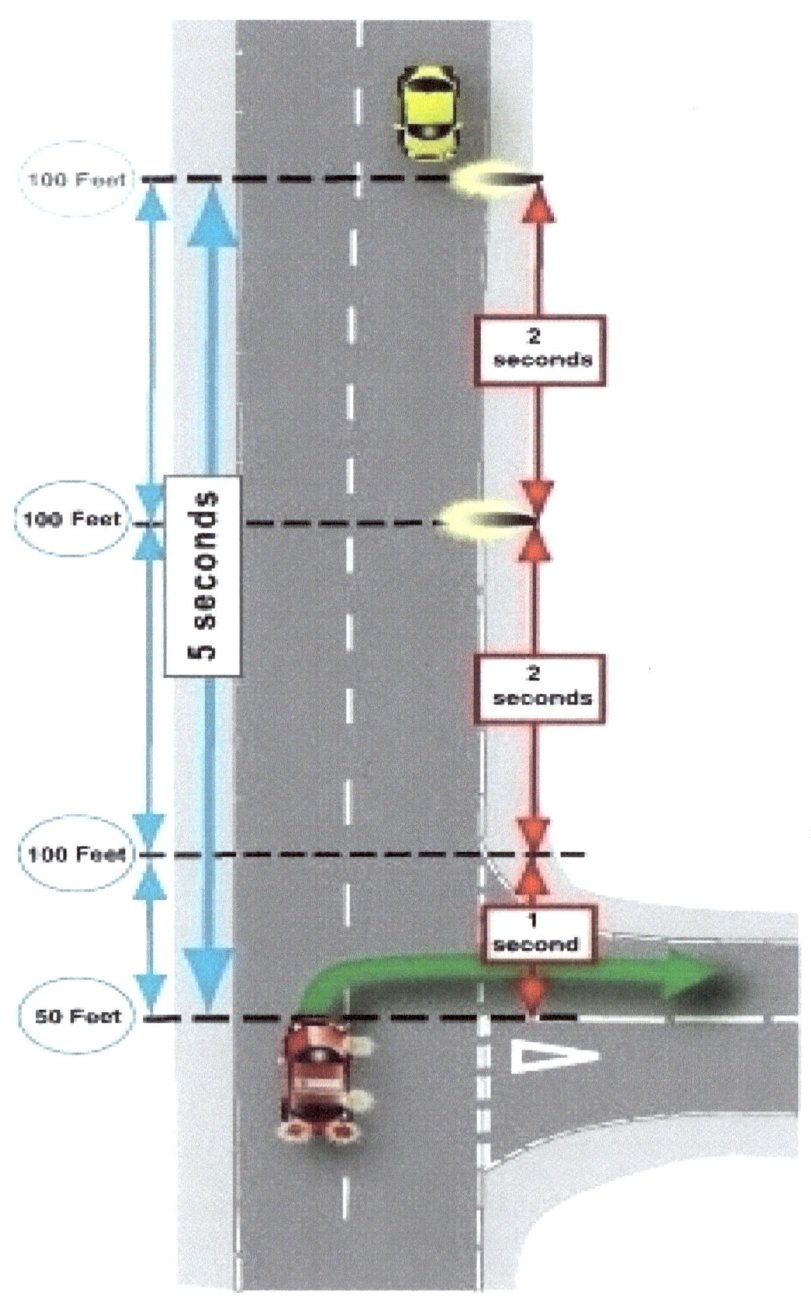

Copyright Bill Bryans, Instructor Training Services, 2009

Part 10

T-Junctions Emerging

'T' Junctions When Emerging

Recognition of the Hazard

Road Signs (100 meters)
- **'Give Way' Signs**
- **'Stop' Signs'**
- **Yellow Box Junctions**
- **Traffic Light Sequence**

White Lines
- **'Give Way Lines' or 'Priority Lines'**
- **'Give Way' Triangle**
- **Hazard Warning Lines in the Side Road**
- **Hazard Warning Lines on the Priority Route**

Gaps in;
- **Walls**
- **Hedges**
- **Buildings**

Buildings
- **Different Shaped Buildings**
- **Different Heights of Buildings**
- **Different Roof Lines**
- **Gabble Ends of Buildings**

Recognition: 'T' Junctions when Emerging

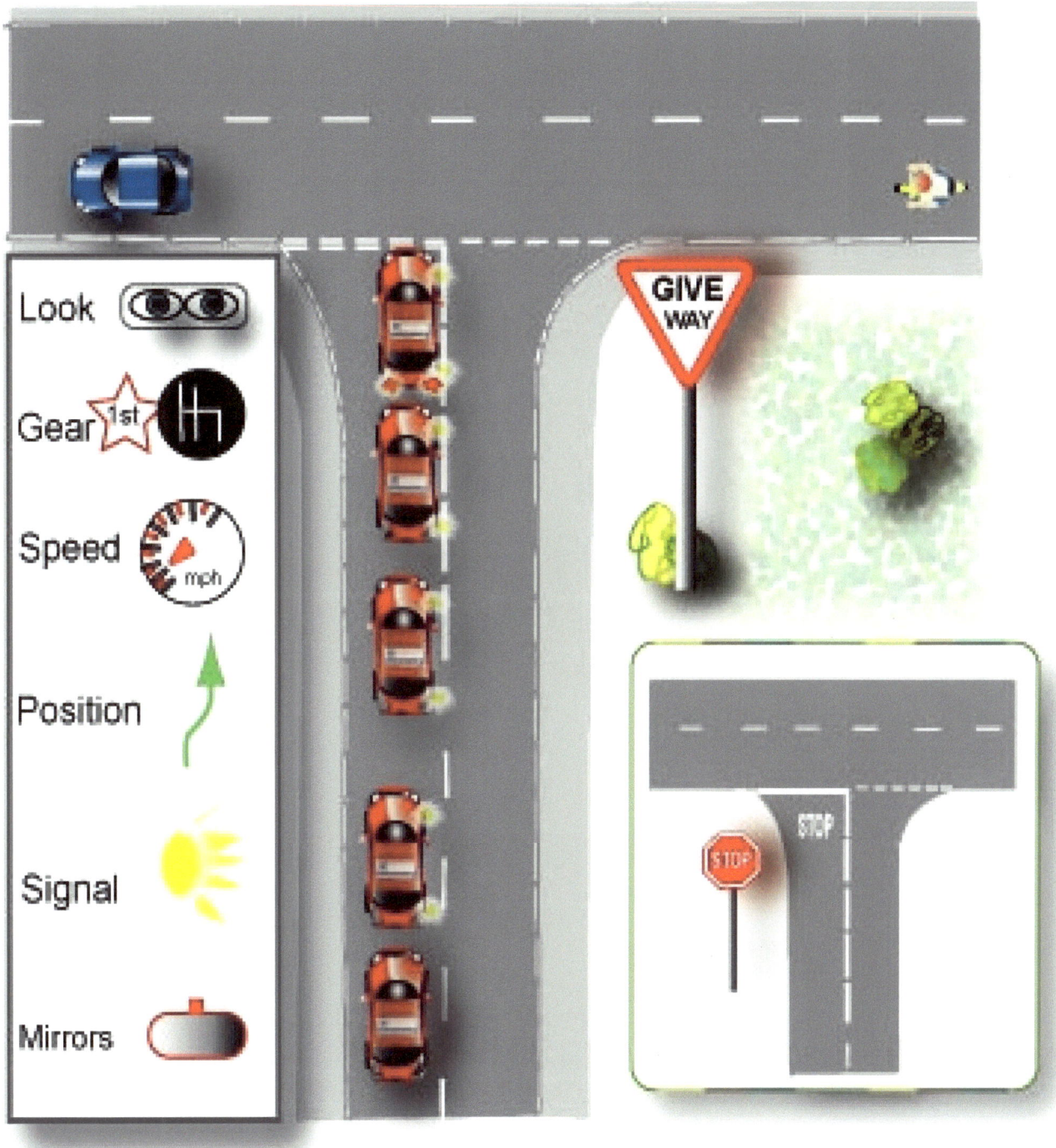

T' Junctions when Emerging.

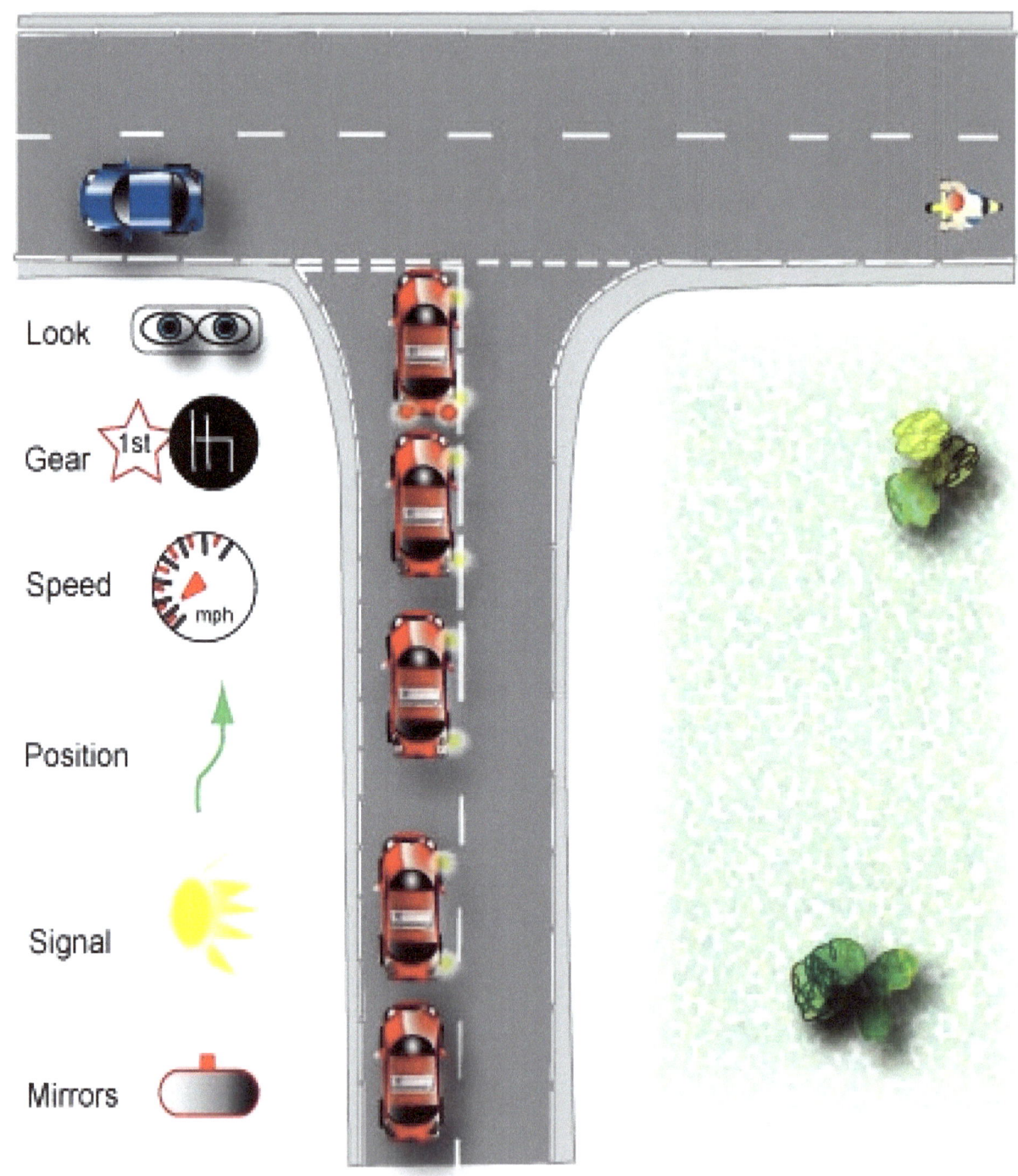

'T' Junctions when Emerging – Crossing a Flow

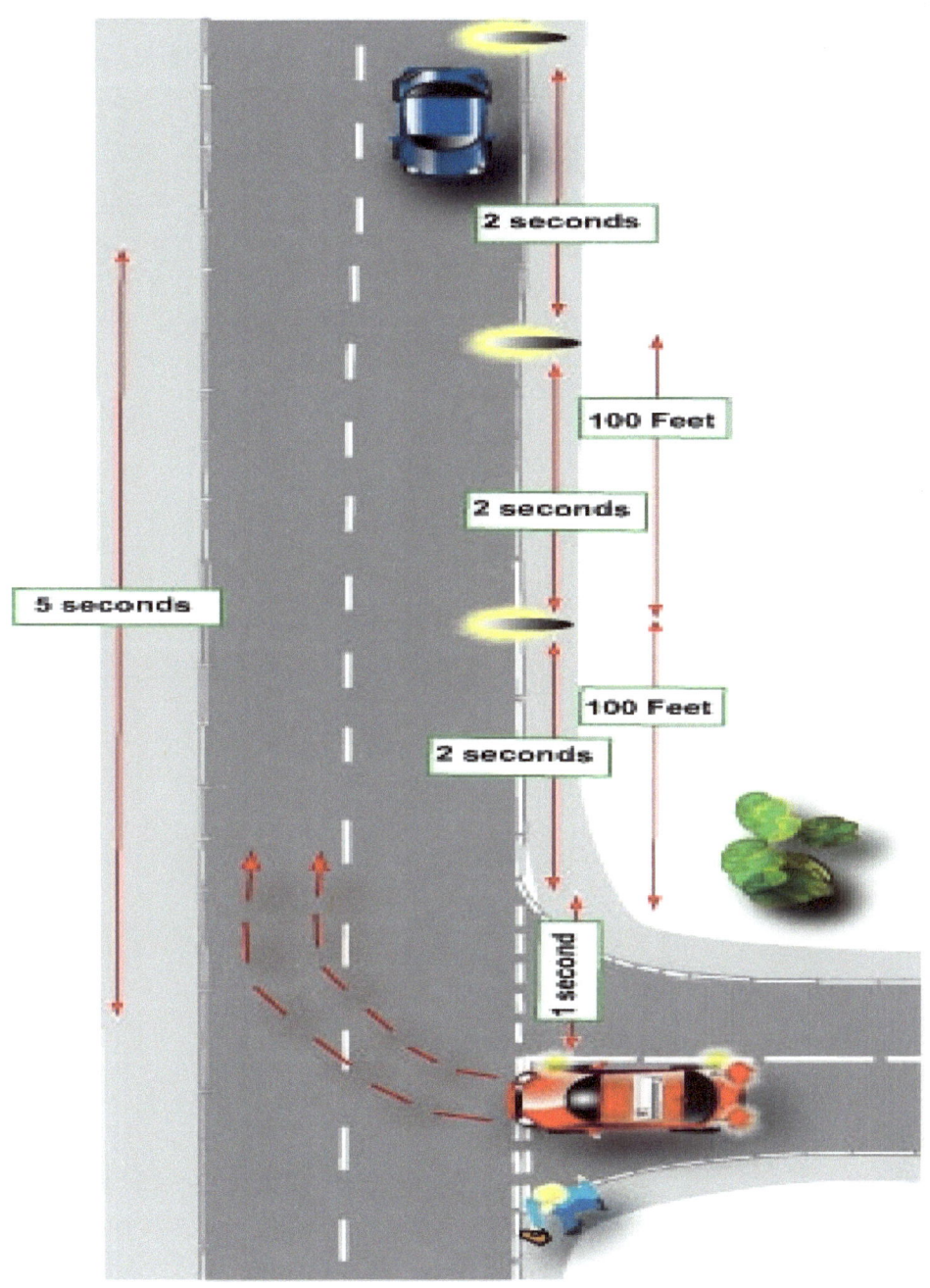

Copyright Bill Bryans, Instructor Training Services, 2009

'T' Junctions when Emerging – Joining a Flow

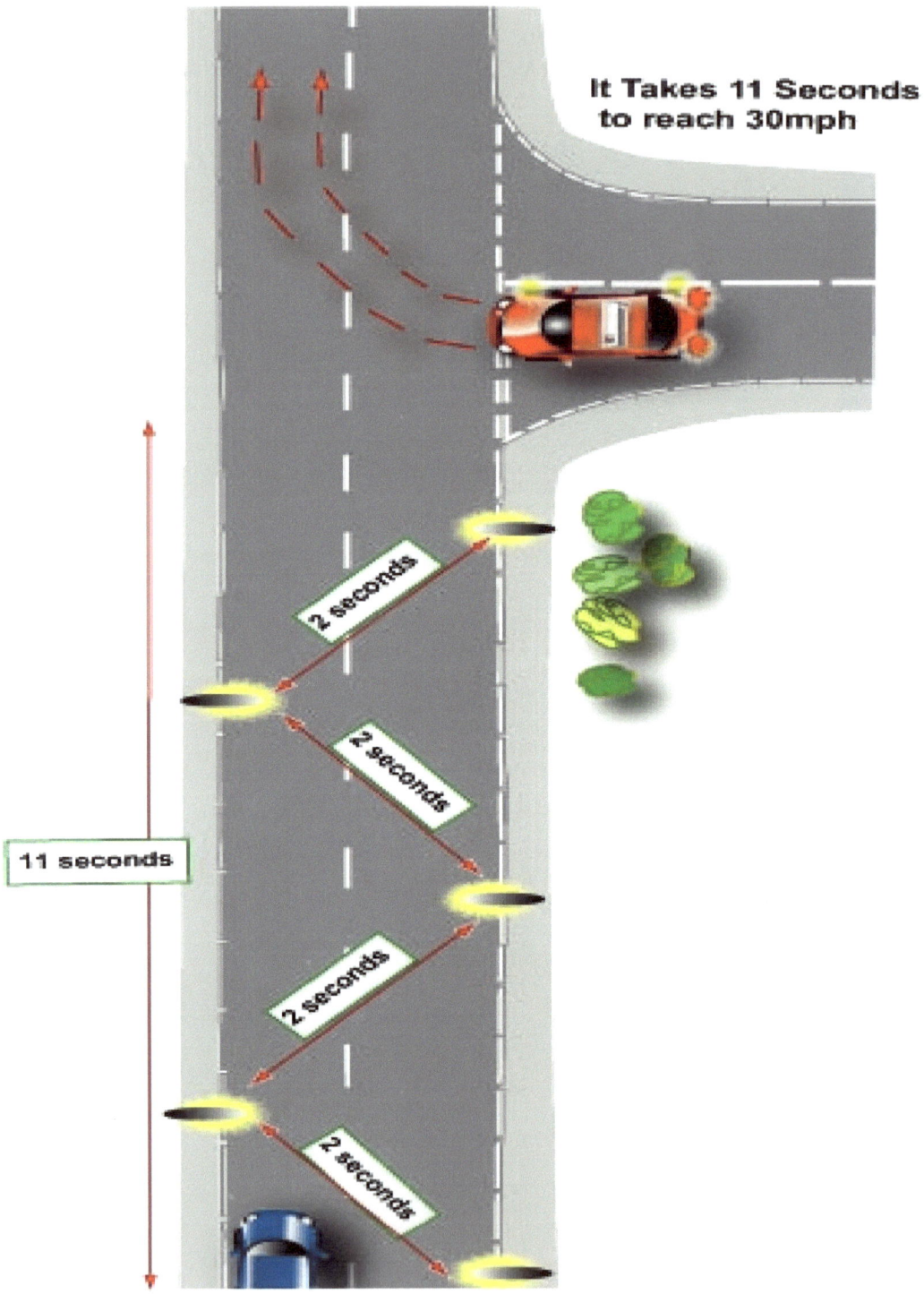

'T' Junctions when Emerging – Dual Carriageways.

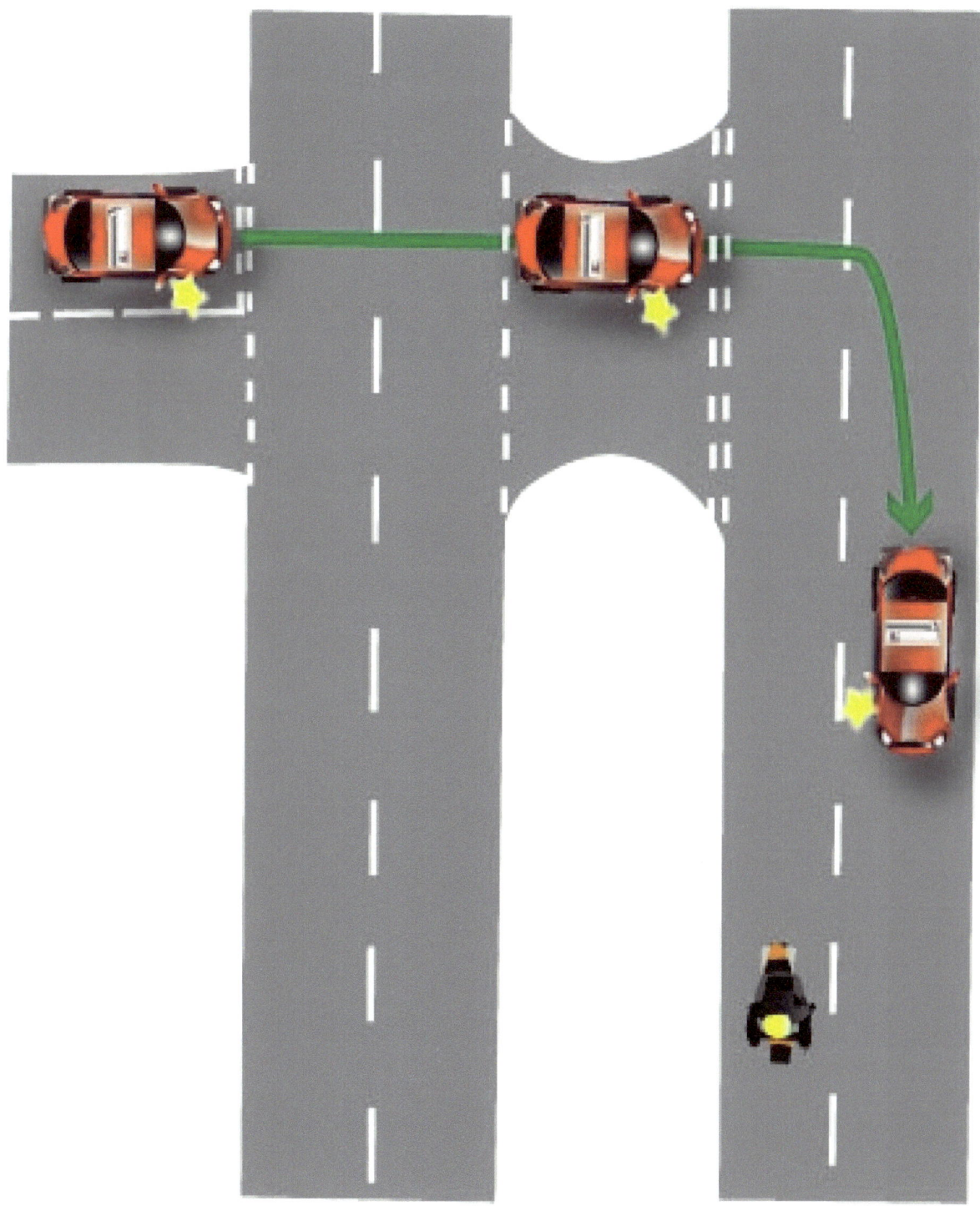

Part 11

Crossroads

Crossroads

Recognition of the Hazard

Road Signs (100 meters)
- 'Give Way' Signs
- 'Stop' Signs'
- Yellow Box Junctions
- Traffic Light Sequence

White Lines
- 'Give Way Lines' or 'Priority Lines'
- 'Give Way' Triangles
- Hazard Warning Lines in the Side Road
- Hazard Warning Lines on the Priority Route

Gaps in;
- Walls
- Hedges
- Buildings

Buildings
- Different Shaped Buildings
- Different Heights of Buildings
- Different Roof Lines
- Gabble Ends of Buildings

Recognition of Marked Crossroads: MS-PSGL

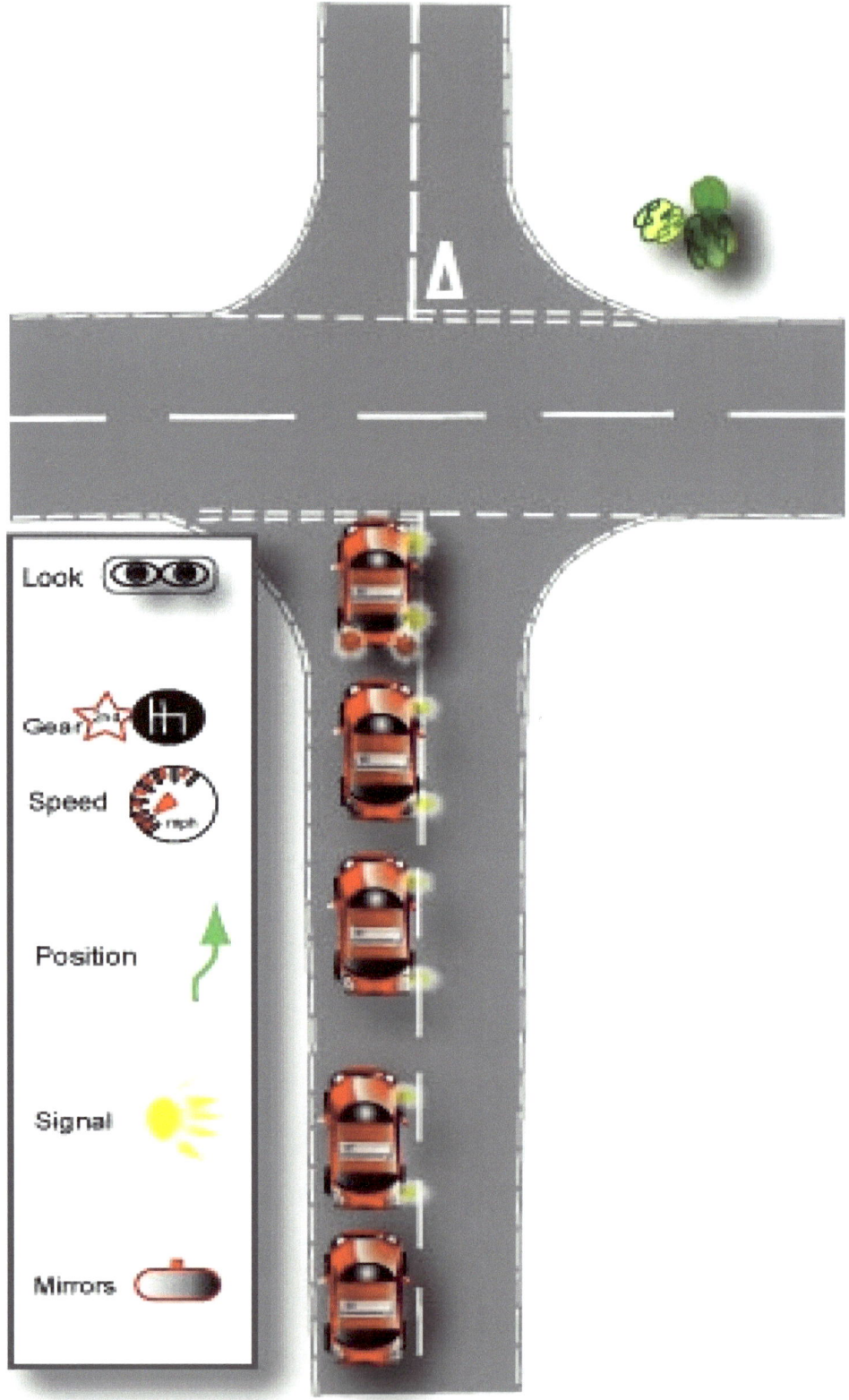

Copyright Bill Bryans, Instructor Training Services, 2009

Recognition of Crossroads: Priority Route Field of Vision

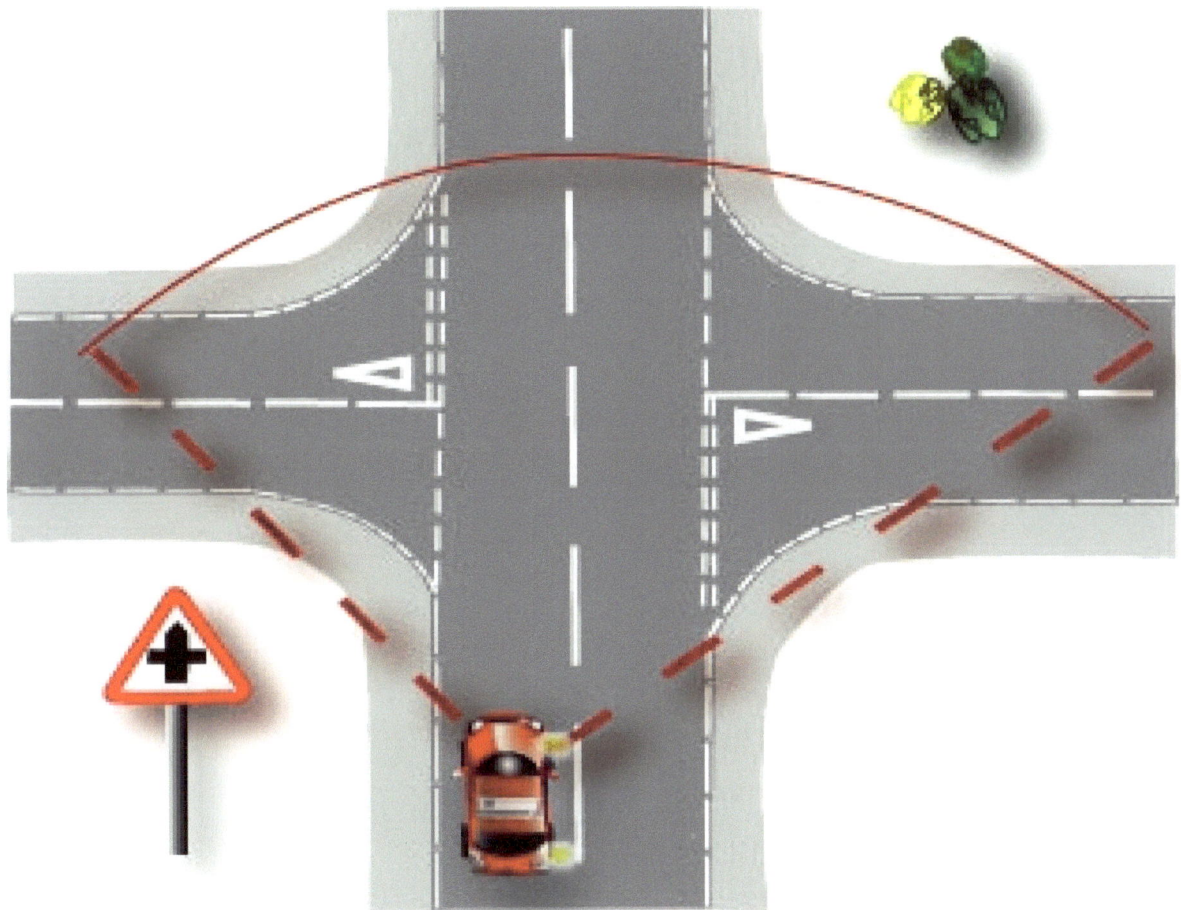

Copyright Bill Bryans, Instructor Training Services, 2009

Recognition of Crossroads: Unmarked

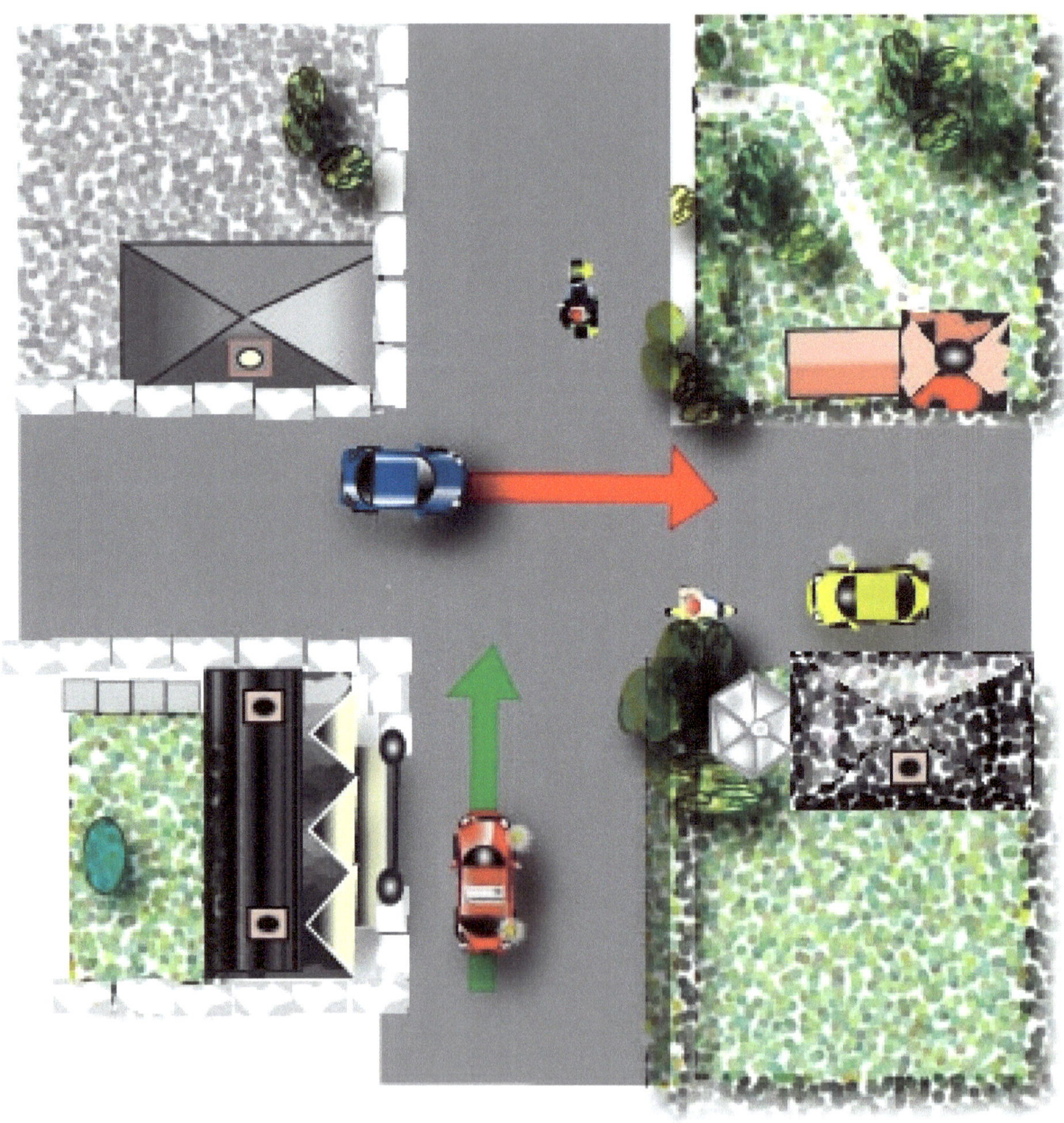

Recognition of Crossroads: Staggered

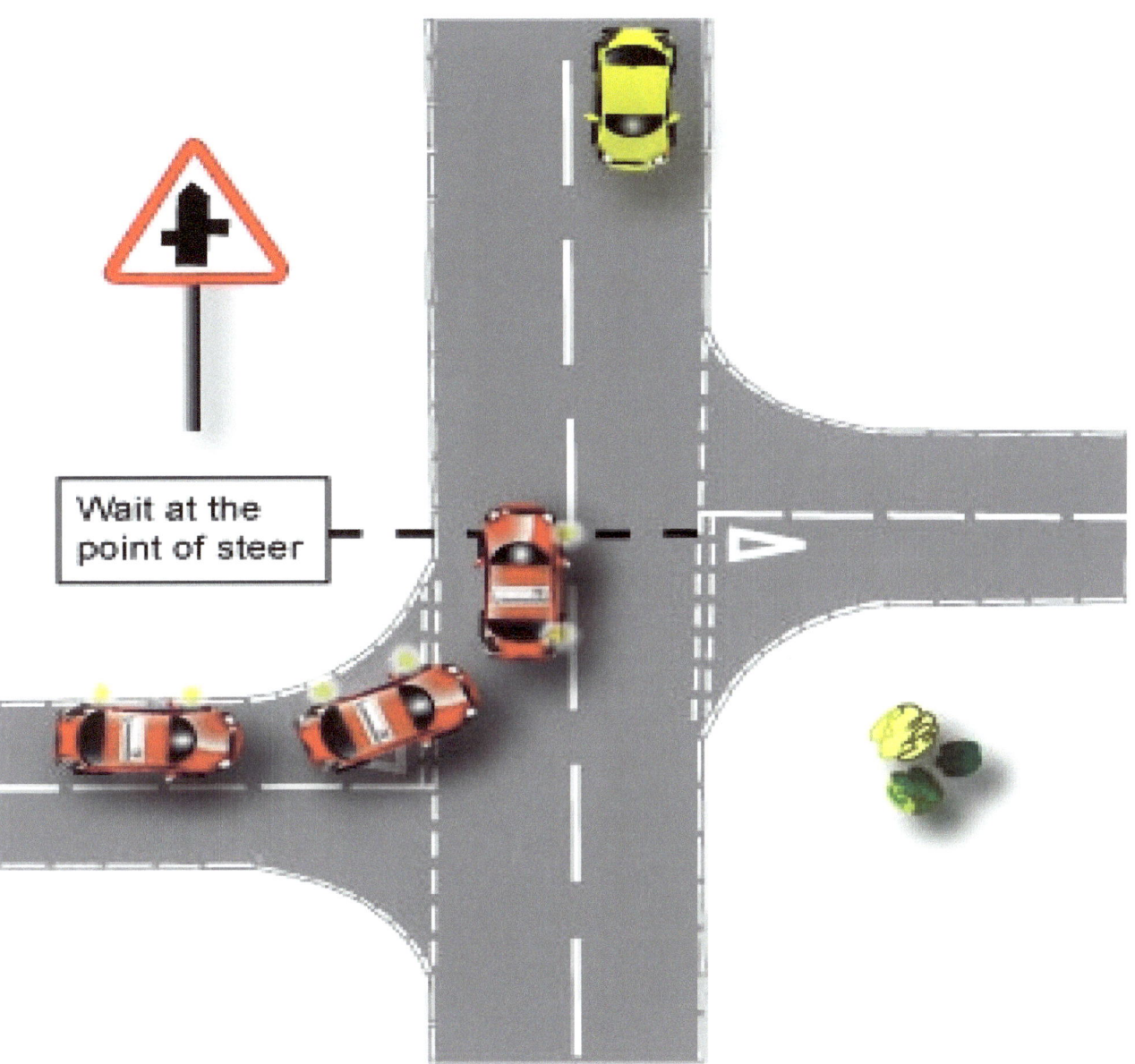

Crossroads: Crossing Traffic

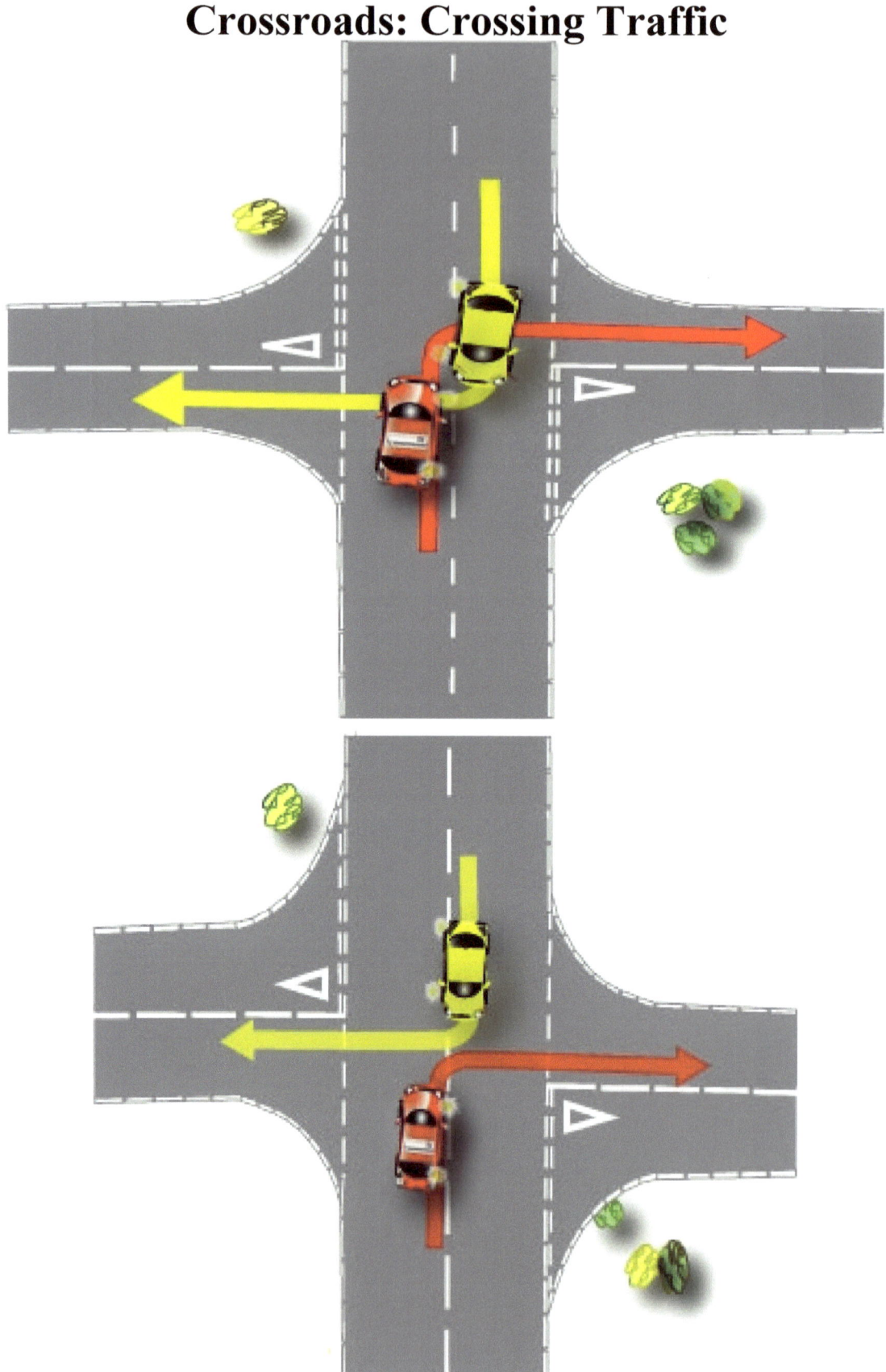

Crossroads: Cut Across Approaching Traffic

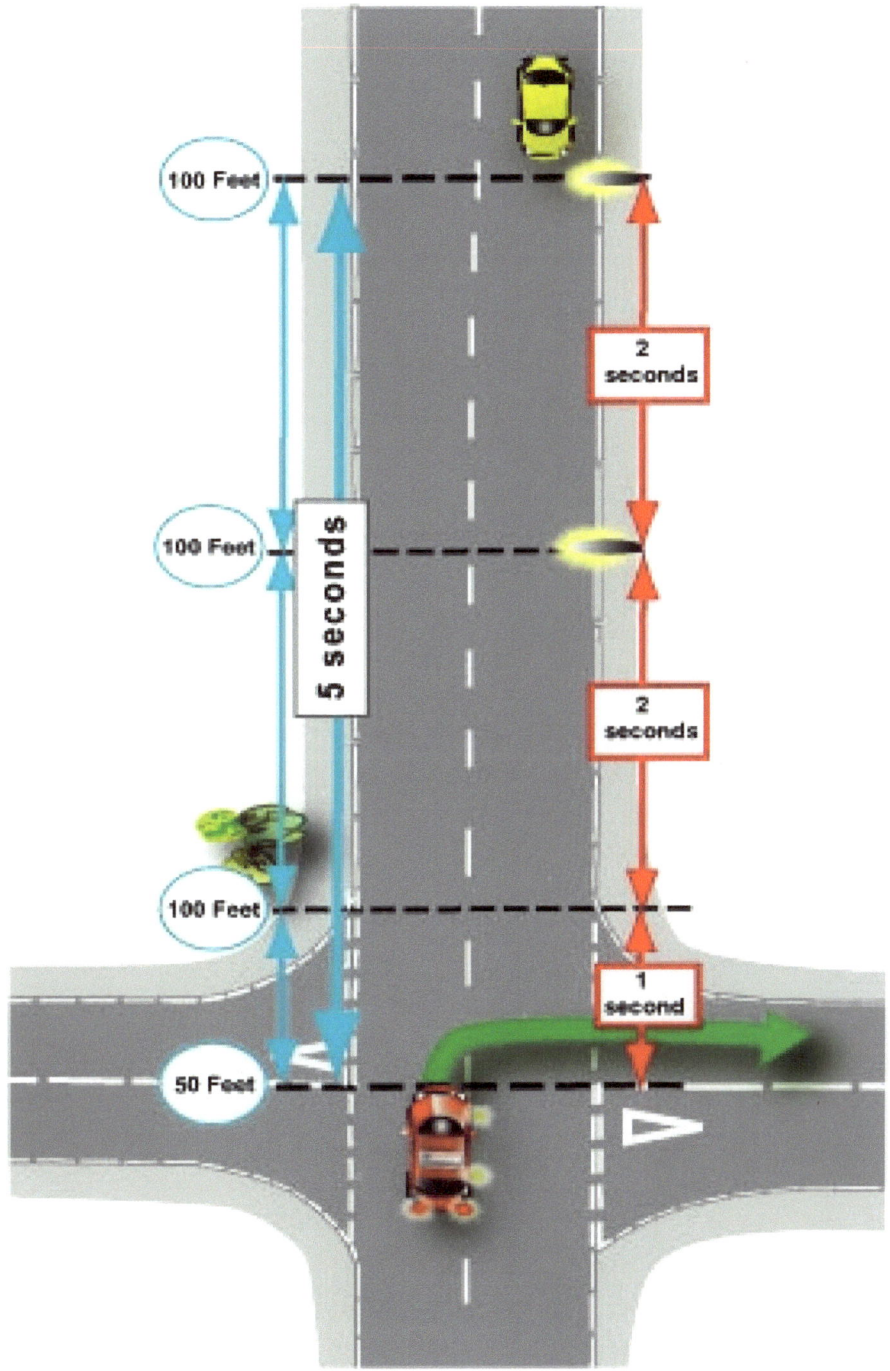

If you have time to walk from one kerb to the other, you have time to drive across

Crossroads: Cut Across Approaching Traffic
Dual Carriageways

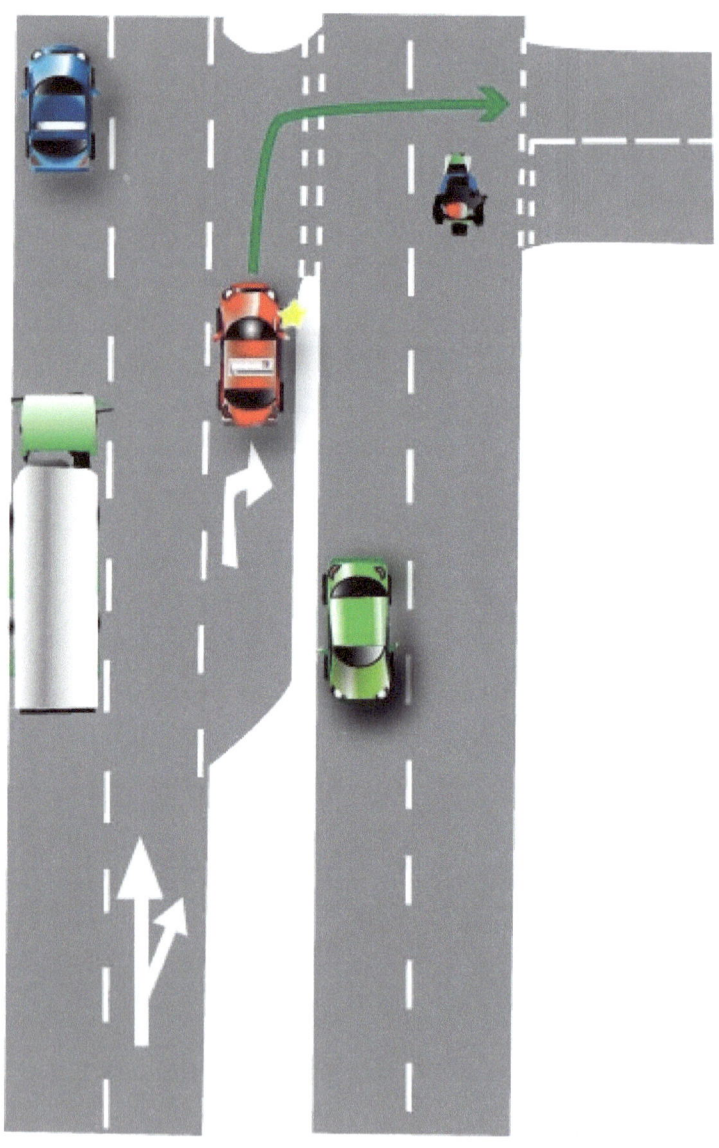

Hazard Recognition Crossroads Trained Stage

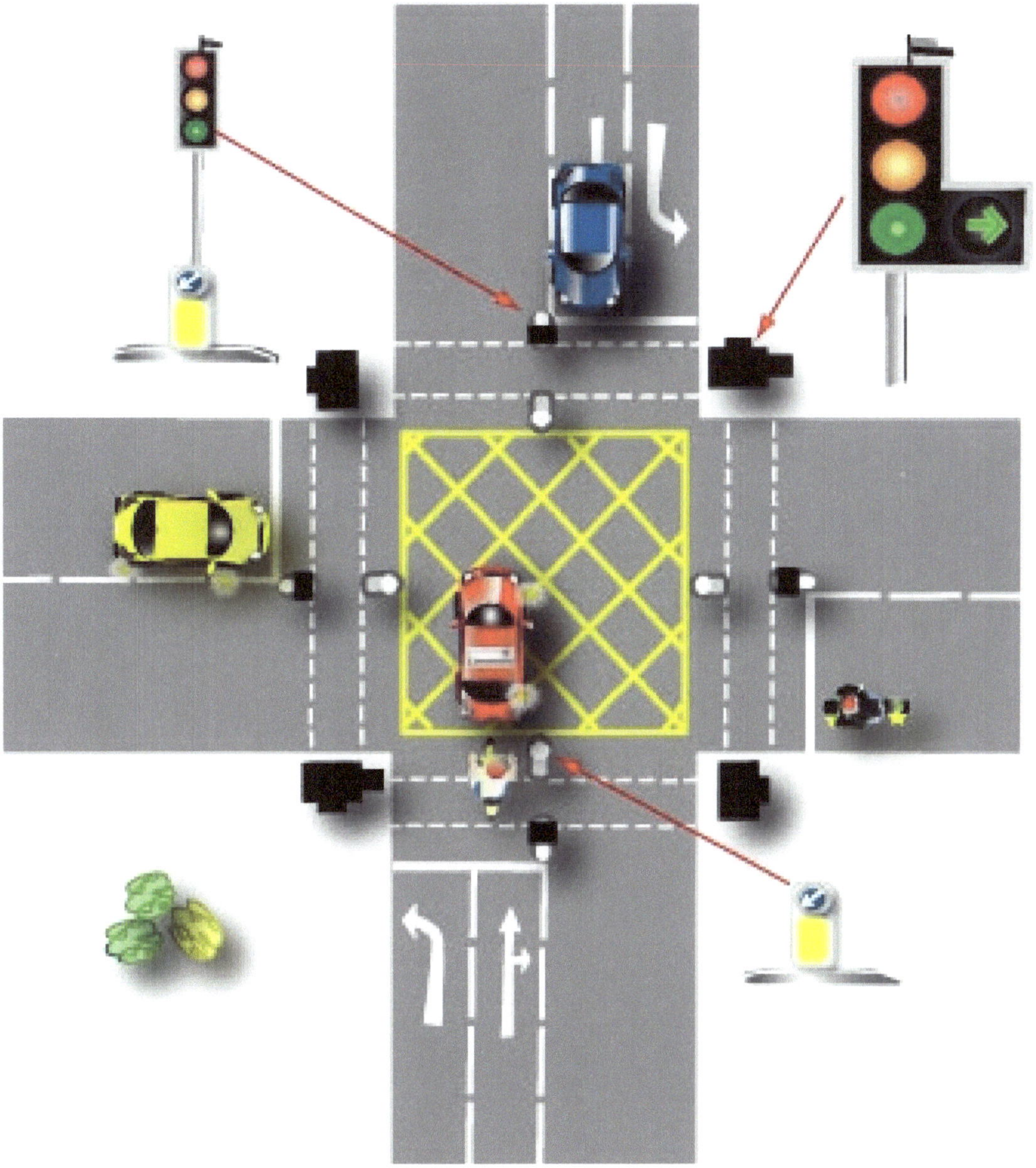

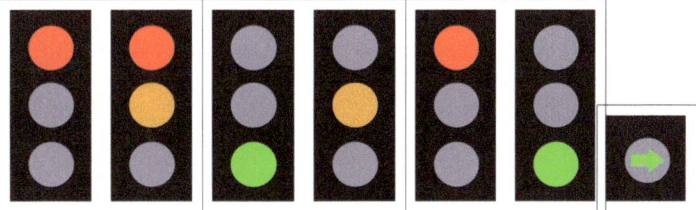

Part 12

Meet Approaching Traffic

Meet Approaching Traffic

Recognition of the Hazard

Road Signs (100 meters)
        Priority Sign with Driver
        Priority Sign with the opposing Driver

White Lines
        'Give Way Lines' on the None Priority Route

Parked vehicles;
        On the Left
        On the Right
        Both Sides

Gaps between Parked Vehicles
        How to use the Gaps

The Anticipation of;
        Other Drivers
        Pedestrians
        Cyclists

Meet Approaching Traffic

Mirrors Signal Position Speed Gear Look.

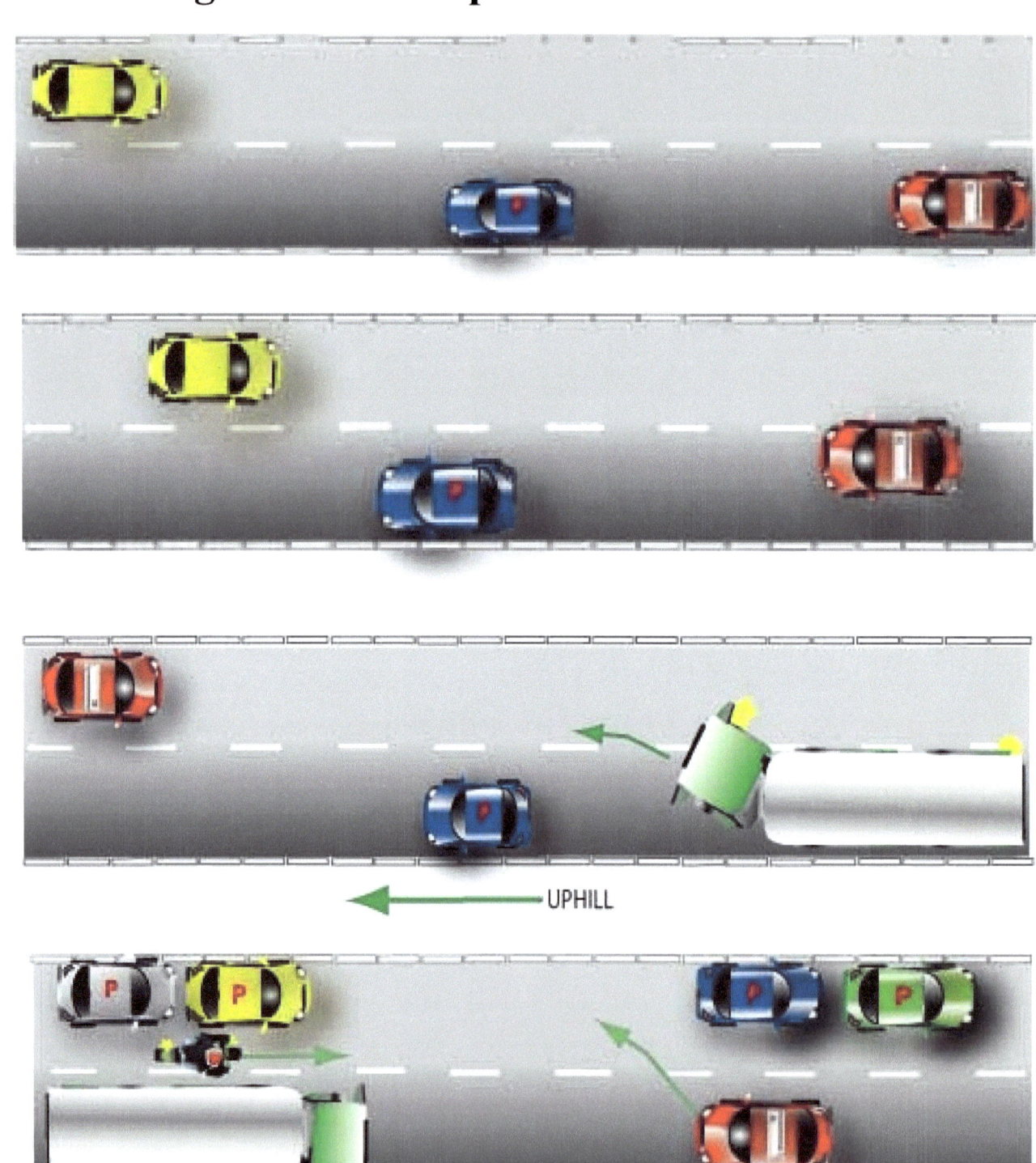

UPHILL

Meet Approaching Traffic

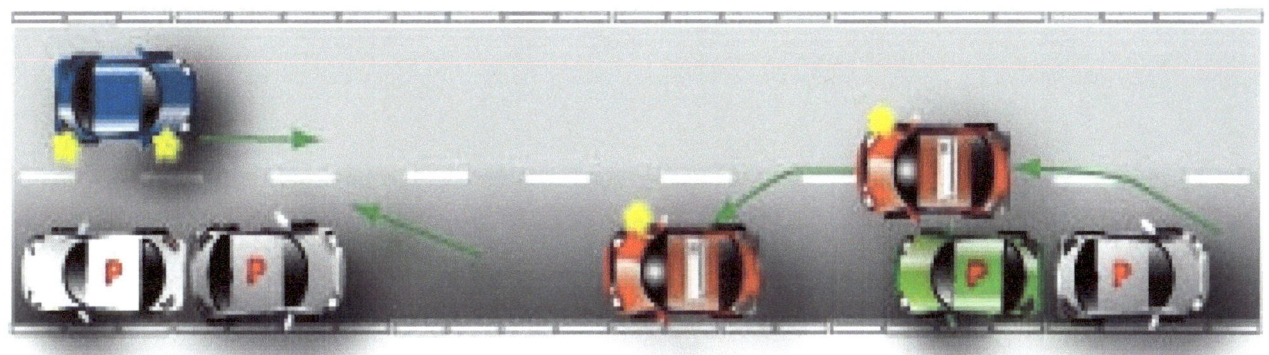

Copyright Bill Bryans, Instructor Training Services, 2009

Meet Approaching Traffic

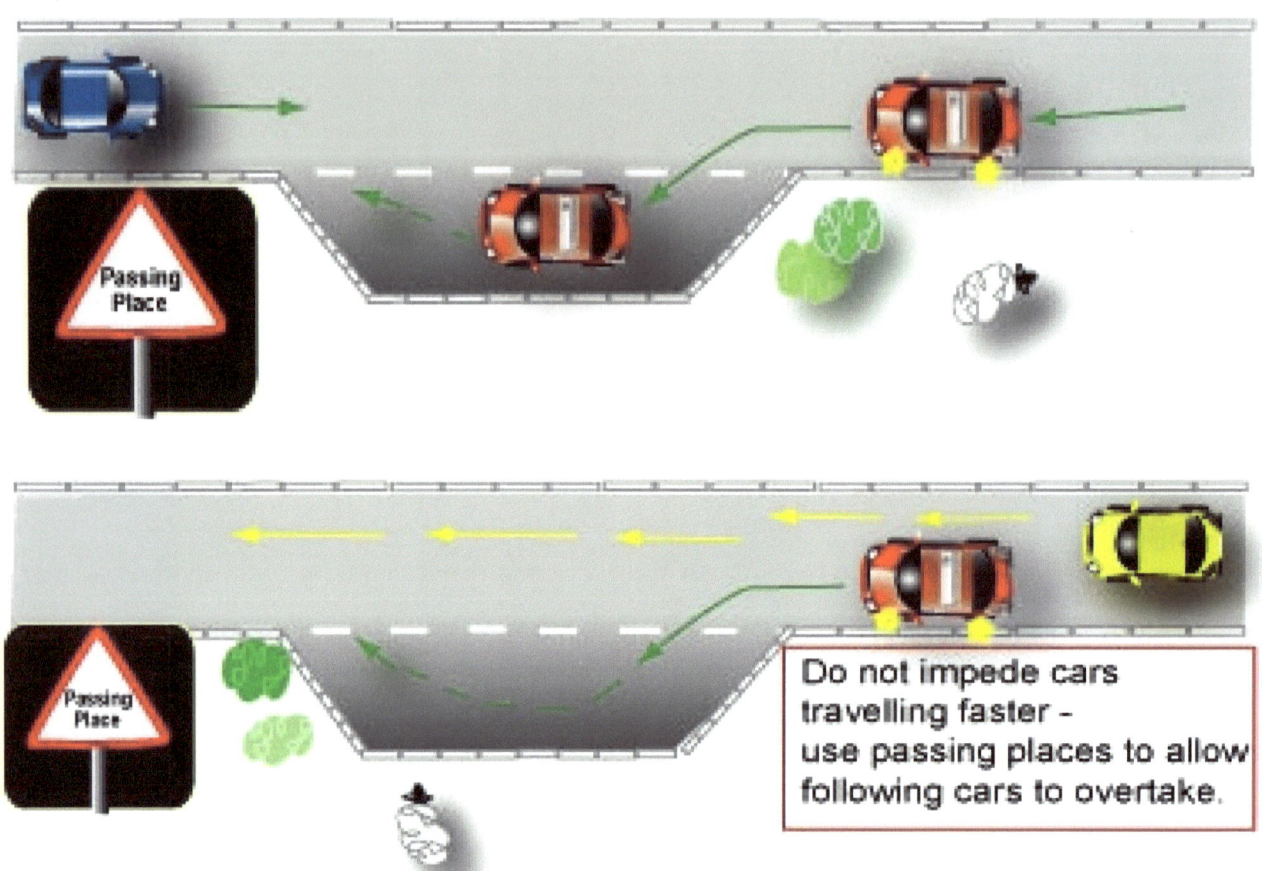

Allow adequate Clearance to Stationary Vehicles

Anticipation of Pedestrians & Cyclists

If the Cyclist falls off, he will

fall at least 6 feet (2 meters)

If the Pedestrian falls over

He/she will fall at least

6 feet (2 metres)

Drive at a speed where you

could stop if necessary.

Copyright Bill Bryans, Instructor Training Services, 2009

Keep a Safe Distance

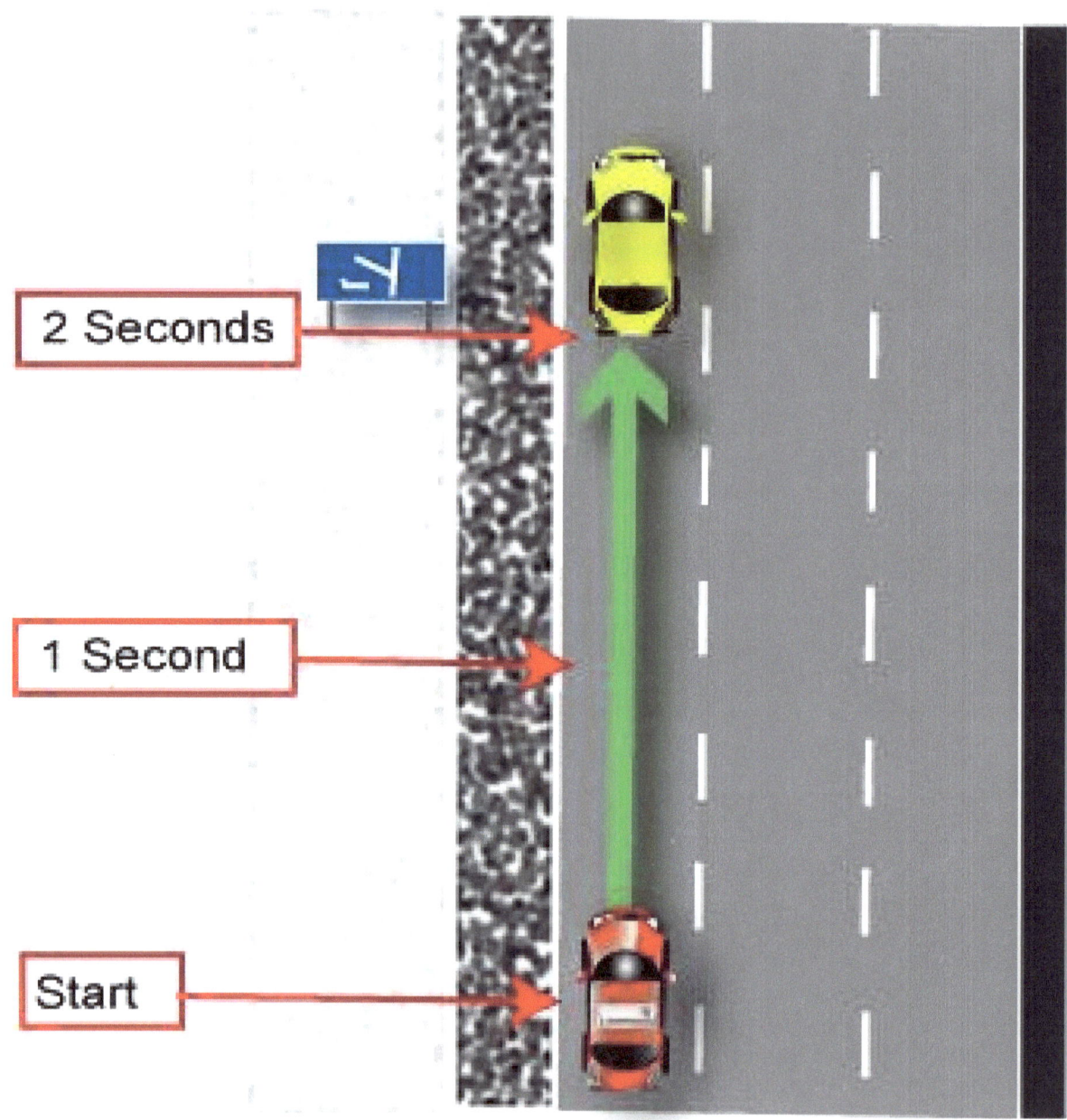

'Only a fool breaks the two second rule' takes two seconds to say

Keep a Safe Distance

When pulling up in traffic you should be able
to see the bottom of the tyres of the car in front

Keep a Safe Distance: The Anticipation of Animals

Horses React Badly to Shadows from Behind

The Anticipation of Animals

Anticipation: Country Driving

Copyright Bill Bryans, Instructor Training Services, 2009

Part 13

Cut Across Approaching Traffic

Cut Across Approaching Traffic

Recognition of the Hazard

Road Signs (100 meters)

    Signs Directional

    Yellow Box Junctions

    'Keep Clear' Written on the Road

    Traffic Light Sequence & Filter Lights

White Lines

    Lane Discipline

Judgment of Approaching Traffic

    Use of Static 'Street Furniture' to judge speed

    "If you have time to walk from one curbstones to the other, you have time to drive across"

    (It takes 5 seconds to walk across a 24.5 foot road)

    Calculating feet per Second (30 mph =45 fps)

    20 mph plus half = 30 fps

    30 mph plus half = 45 fps

    40 mph plus half = 60 fps

Cut Across Approaching Traffic MS-PSGL

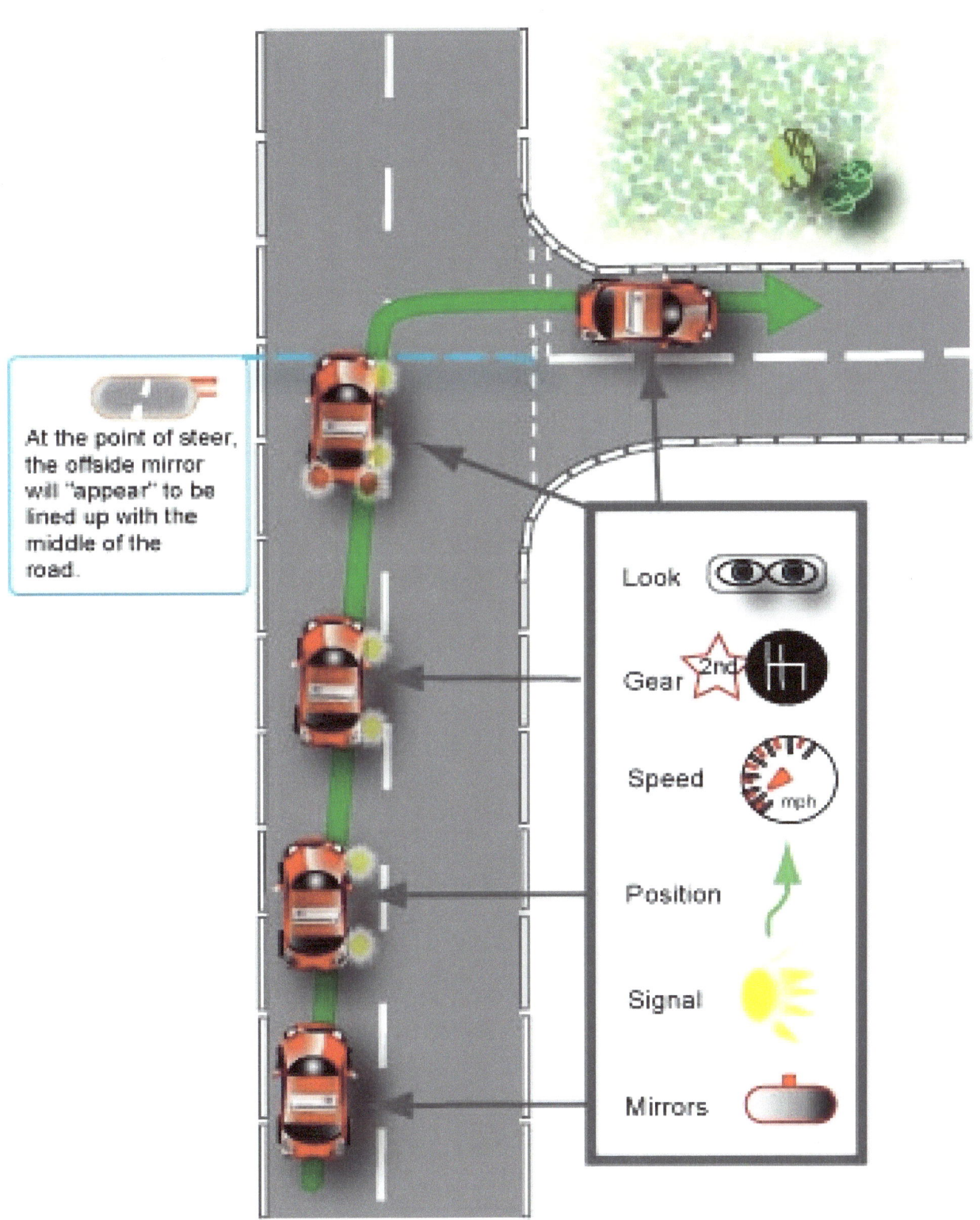

Cut Across Approaching Traffic - Crossroads:

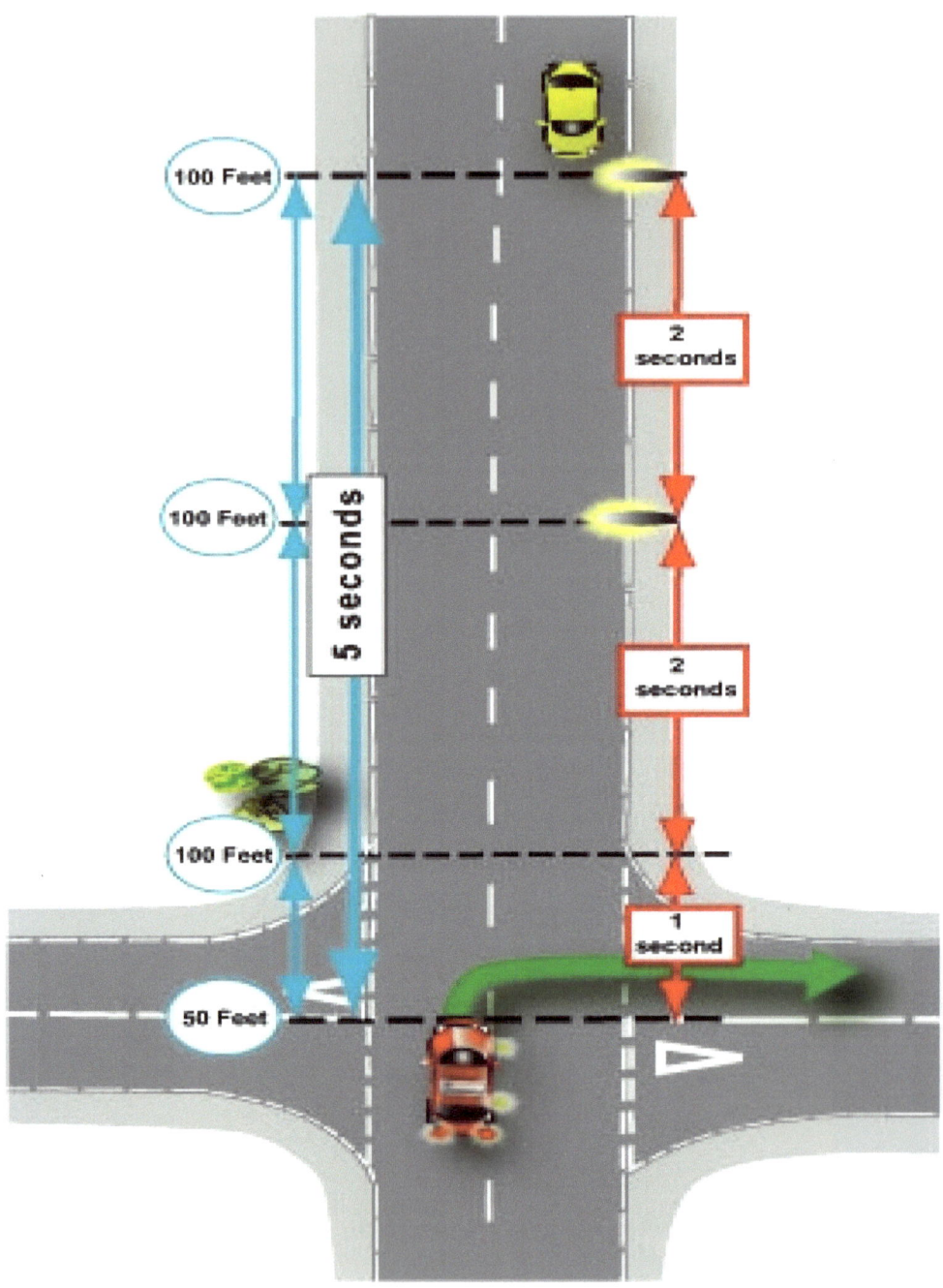

**If you have time to walk from one kerb
to the other, you have time to drive across**

Copyright Bill Bryans, Instructor Training Services, 2009

Cut Across Approaching Traffic

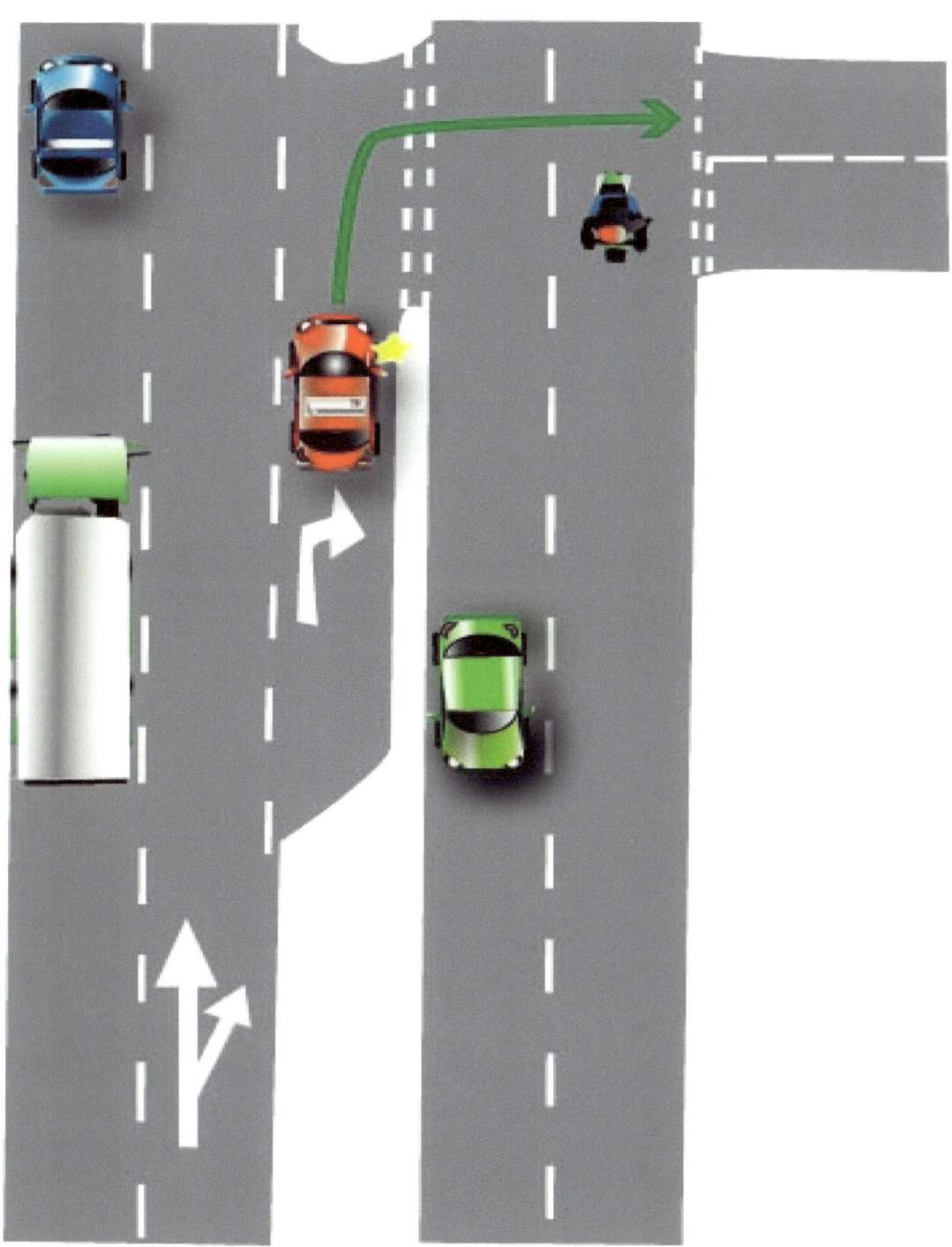

Cut Across Approaching Traffic - Crossroads:

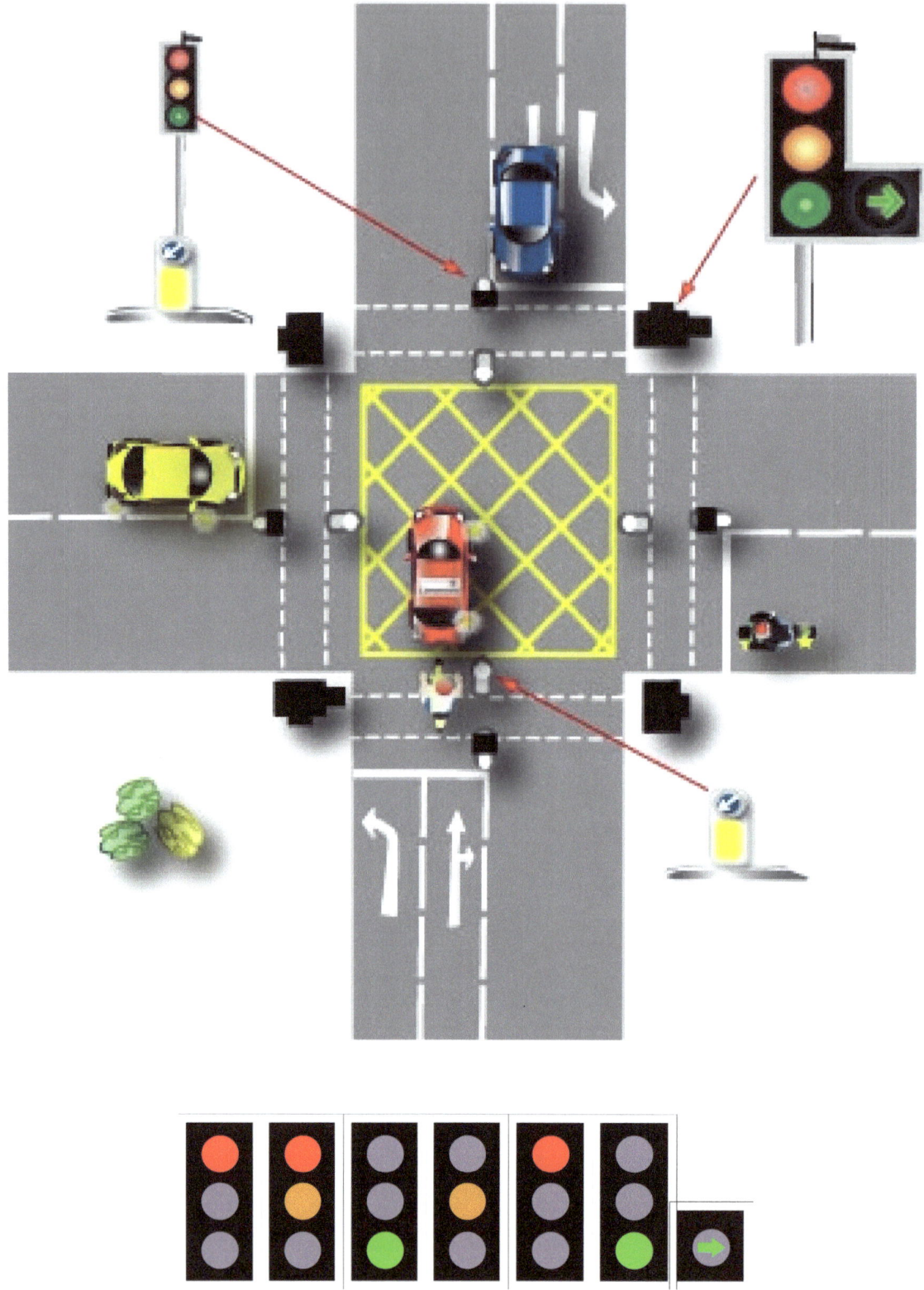

Part 14

Overtaking

Recognition of the Hazard Overtaking

Road Signs (100 meters)
Signs No Overtaking

White Lines
'Solid' white centre lines
'Broken' white centre lines

Lane Discipline on Dual Carriageways
Two Lanes
Three or More Lanes
Lane Discipline requirements of Buses & Lorries

Overtaking on Bends
Left Bends (Target vehicle causes a 'Blind Spot')
Right Bends (Long downhill Right Bends with a constant, uncluttered, view may be possible)

Speed Limits

Lorries	40 mph	50 mph	60 mph
Buses	50 mph	60 mph	70 mph
Cars	60 mph	70 mph	70 mph

NB. Since 1997 all Buses and Lorries manufactured within the EEC are restricted to a maximum of 100 kph – 60 mph

Judgment of Approaching Traffic
The Minimum Differential between the Target vehicle and the Trainees speed (20 mph)

Overtaking: Procedure

Mirrors, Position, Gear, Speed, Look - Mirrors, Signal, Maneuver

A Quick Sideways Glance,

When Overtaking and changing lanes

Take a Quick Sideways Glance

Copyright Bill Bryans, Instructor Training Services, 2009

Overtaking:

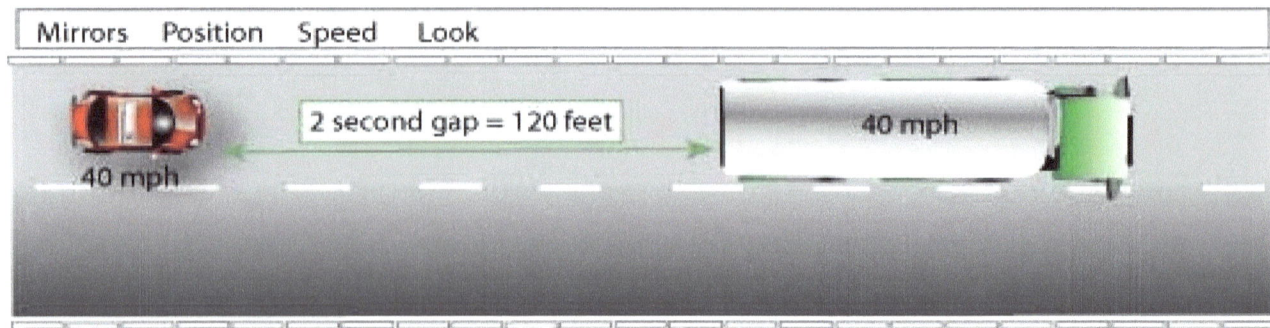

When following another vehicle on the open road, the training vehicle should be the full thinking and braking distance behind, or the '2 second rule', which is the same. (40 mph + 20= 60 feet per second x 2 seconds= 120 feet)

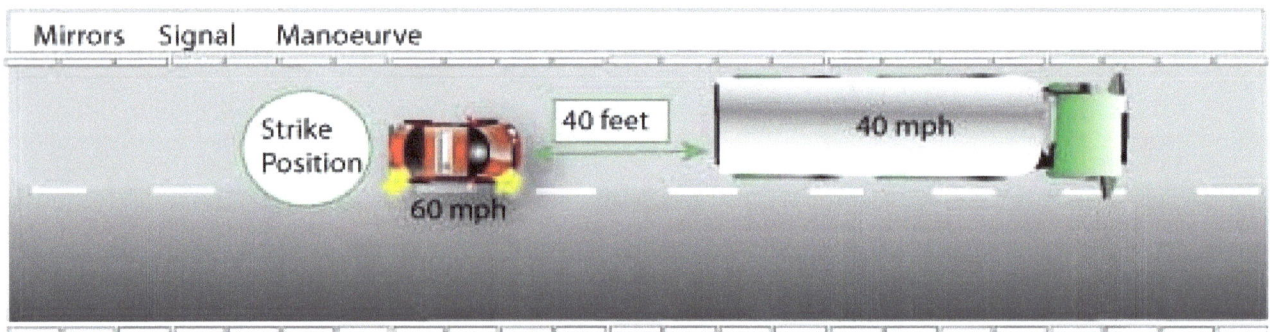

When the training vehicle moves forward to the 'Strike Point' it should not get any closer than the 'Thinking Distance' of 40 feet.

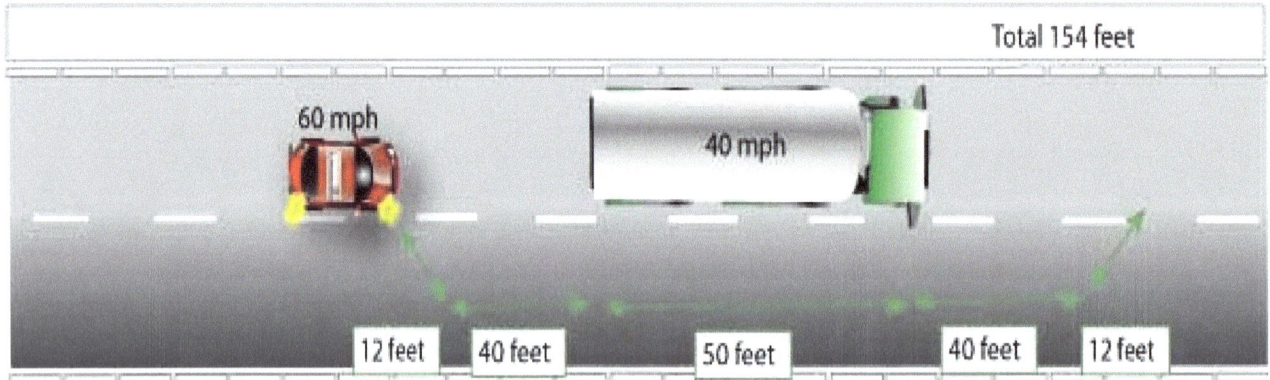

The 'Speed Differential' between the Strike vehicle and the Target vehicle is what is important; 20 mph is usually the minimum – 5 seconds. 10 mph differential is too little because it would take over 10 seconds to overtake a lorry.
(10 mph + 5 = 15 feet per second divided into 154 feet = 10.2 seconds)
(20 mph + 10=30 feet per second divided into 154 feet = 5.1 seconds)

Copyright Bill Bryans, Instructor Training Services, 2009

Overtaking

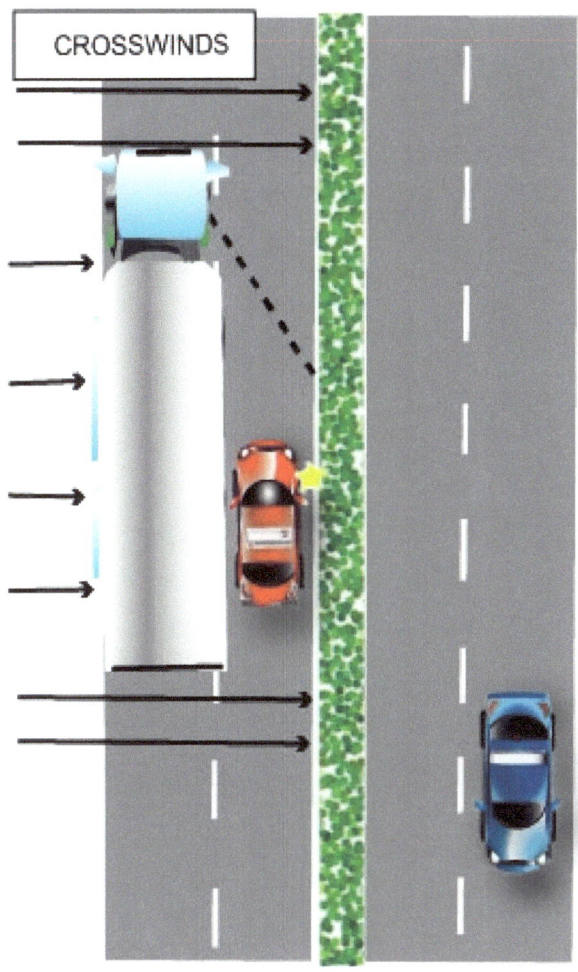

The prevalent wind in Great Britain is from the West, so drivers are most in danger when driving North

*Do not enter the danger zone until the Motorcyclist has 'cleared' the lorry.
If the Motorcyclist cannot break through the 'Bow-wave', you would not have an 'Escape Route'!

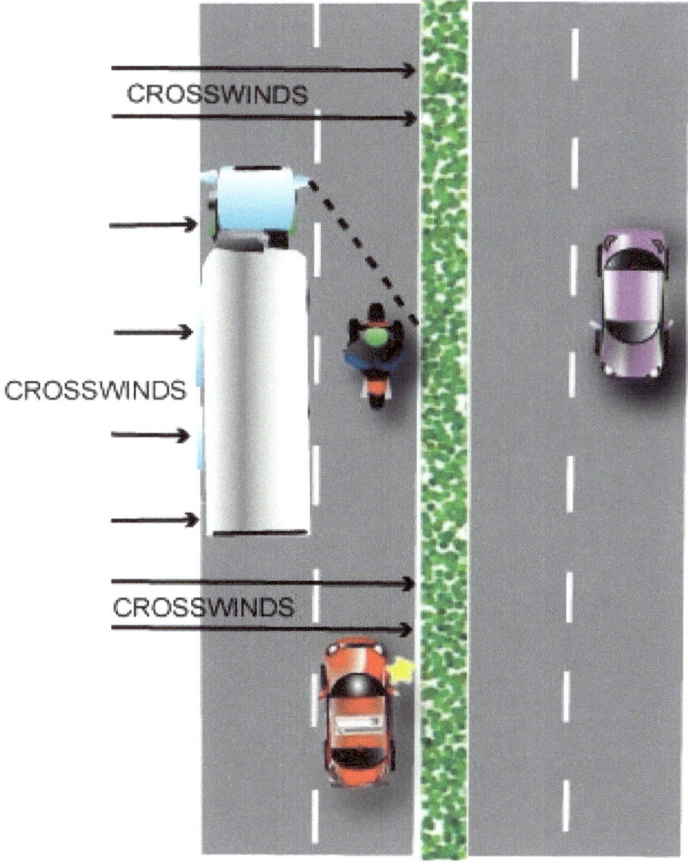

Copyright Bill Bryans, Instructor Training Services, 2009

Overtaking: Escape Routes

No 'Escape Route'   **'Escape Route'**

Copyright Bill Bryans, Instructor Training Services, 2009

Overtaking: Escape Routes

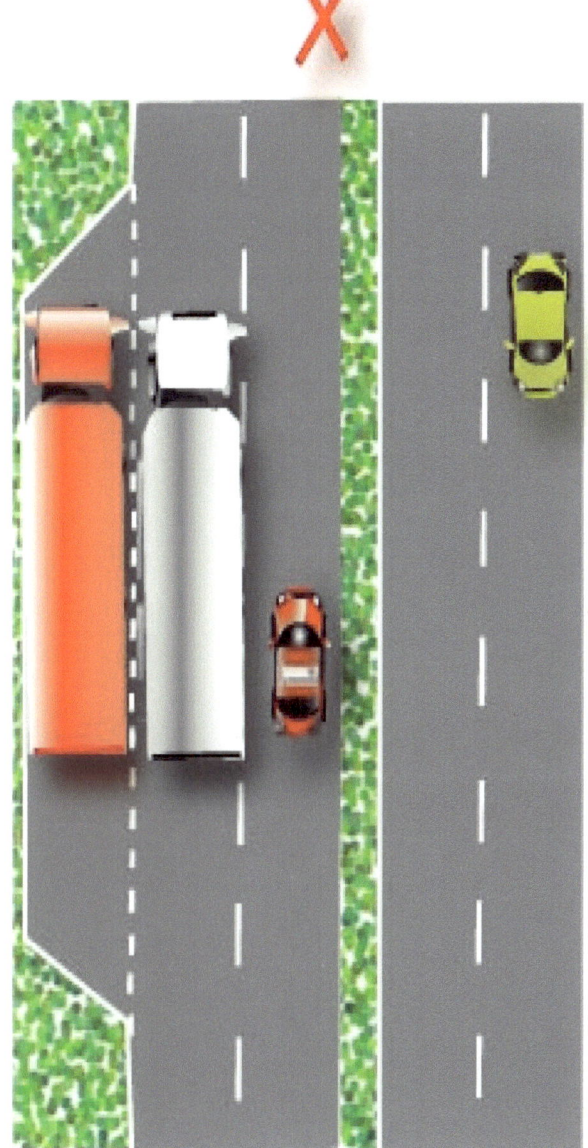

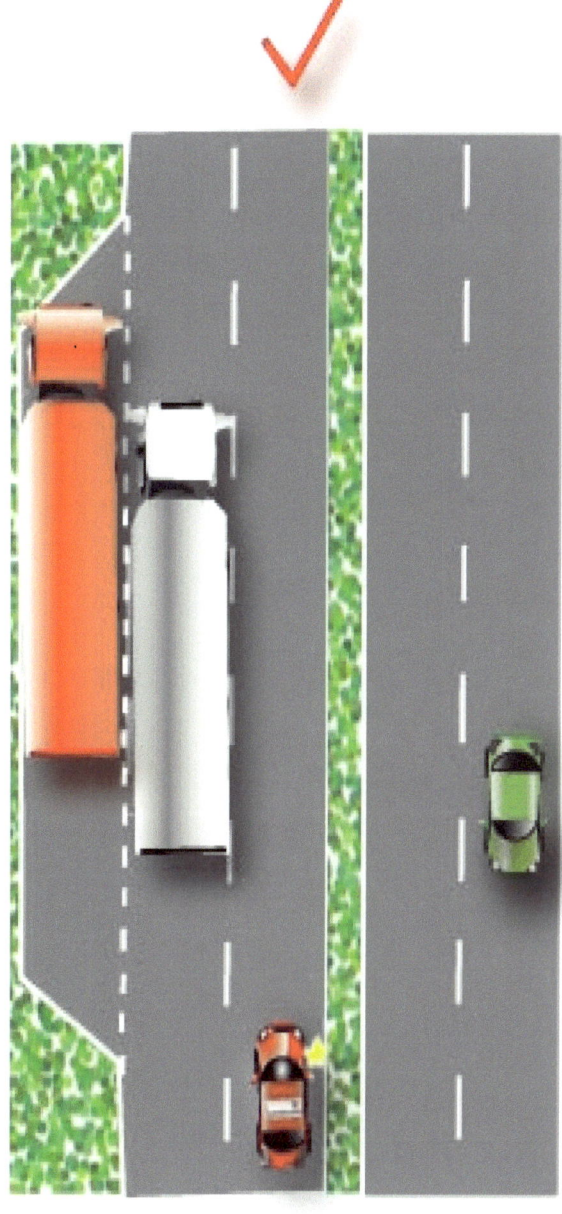

No 'Escape Route'   **'Escape Route'**

Overtaking: The Anticipation of Animals

Horses Shy Away from Shadows from Behind

Allow adequate Distance to Stationary vehicles

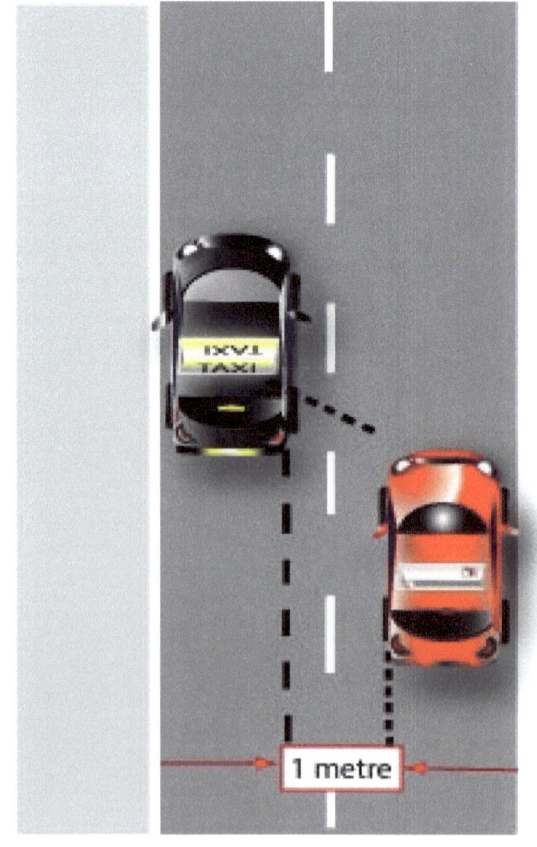

Copyright Bill Bryans, Instructor Training Services, 2009

Anticipation of Animals

Anticipation: Country Driving

Overtaking: Keep a Safe Distance

Overtaking Cyclists

Passing Pedestrians

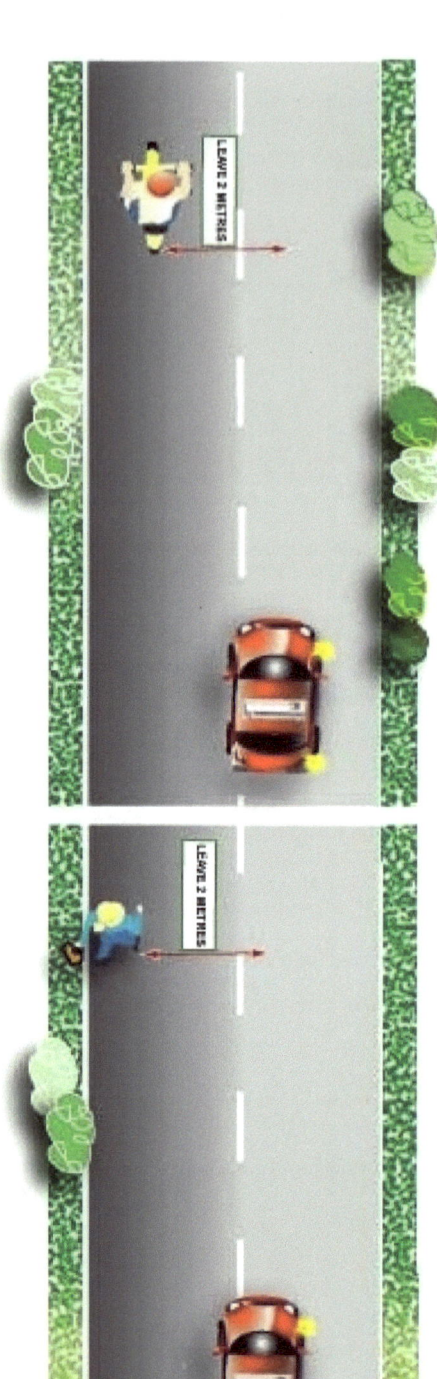

Part 15

Pedestrian Crossings

Pedestrian Crossings

Hazard Recognition

Road Signs (100 meters)

- Concealed Pedestrian Crossing (Usually a Zebra)
- Concealed Pelican Crossing (Warning of a Concealed Traffic Light Sign)
- Concealed Puffin Crossing (Warning of a Concealed Traffic Light Sign)
- Toucan Crossing (Cyclist Warning Sign)
- Equestrian Crossing (Horse & Rider Sign)

White Lines

- 'Zig Zag' White Lines on the Approach
- (No Overtaking, No Parking & Why)

Lane Discipline on Dual Lanes & One Way Systems

- Don't Change Lanes on the Late Approach
- (Lack of traction in the event of an Emergency)

Traffic Lights

- Sequence at Pelican Lights (and why)
- Sequence at all other Crossings (and why)

Anticipation of Crossings

- Blocks of Flats
- Church Spires (Primary Schools)
- Crossroads & Town Centers

Copyright Bill Bryans, Instructor Training, 2009

Pedestrian Crossings - Pelican Crossing

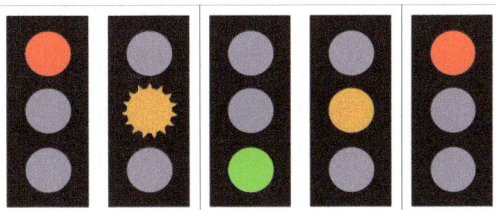

Pedestrian Crossings: Puffin Crossing

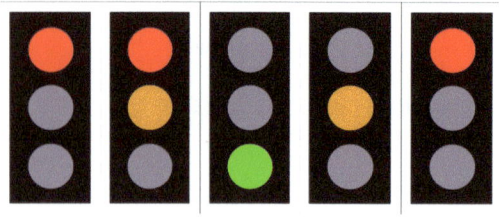

Pedestrian Crossings: Toucan Crossing

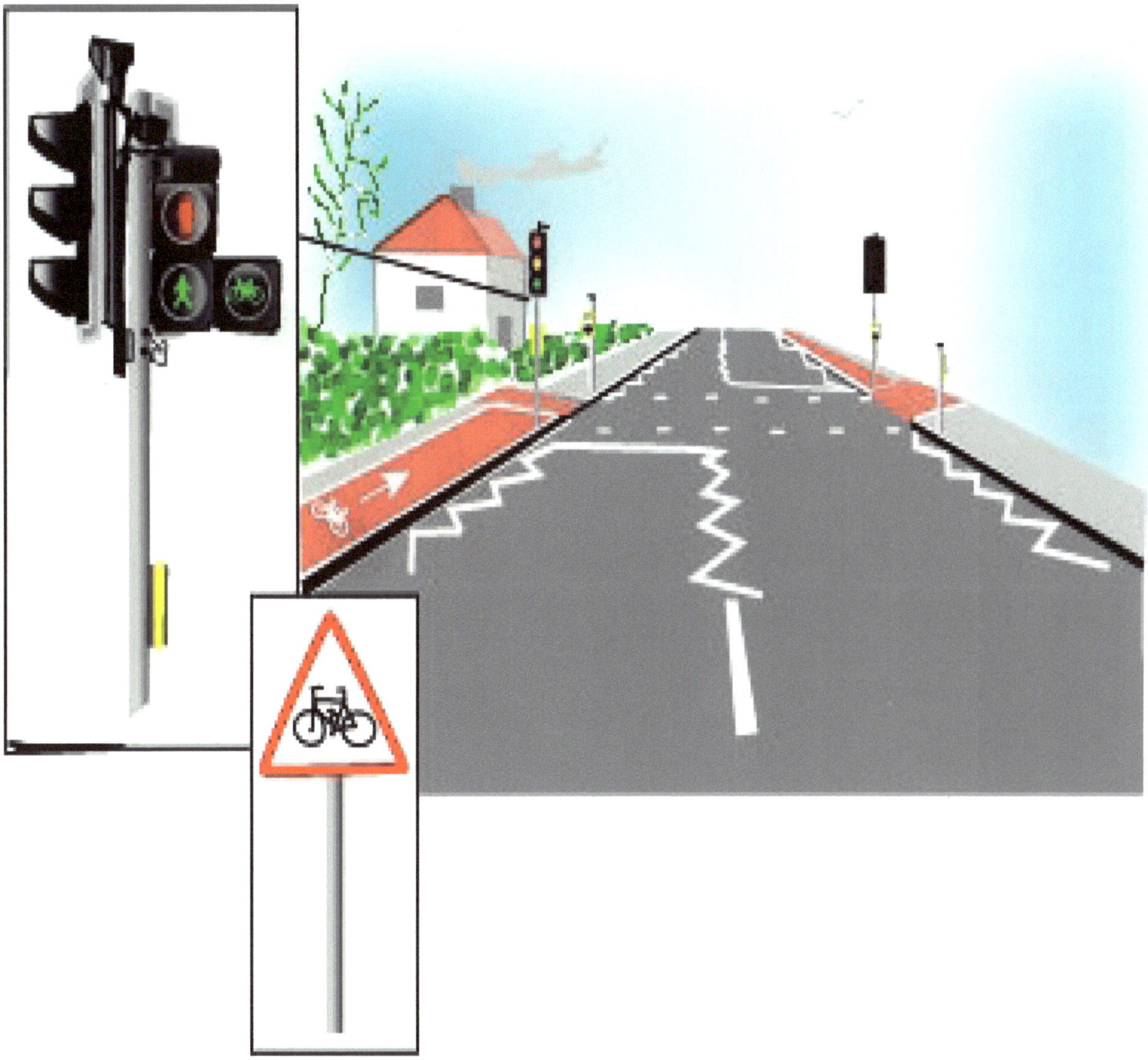

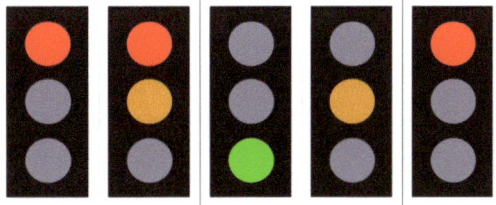

Pedestrian Crossings: Pegasus Crossing

Pedestrian Crossings: Zebra Crossing

Pedestrian Crossings: Traffic Island

Part 16

Signals both by Arm & Indicator

& School Crossing Wardens

Signals: Signals by Arm & Indicator

School Crossing Warden Signals

1. Sign Upside Down ……….Not Ready to Cross
2. Sign Side ways ……………Barrier to Stop Children crossing
3. Sign Held Up High ……….Children Ready to Cross
   Vehicles must prepare to Stop!
4. Sign Extended Out ………..All Vehicles Must Stop!

Copyright Bill Bryans, Instructor Training Services, 2009

Part 17

Roundabouts

Roundabouts

Hazard Recognition

Road Signs Single or Double Lane Road (100 meters)
- Roundabout Warning Sign
- Mini-Roundabouts Warning Sign

Road Signs Dual Carriageways
- Directional Signs (in Green) Half a mile before
- Directional Signs repeated at 400 meters
- Countdown Markers (300 meters)

White Lines
- 'Give Way' Line at the entry
- 'Give Way' Lines, occasionally after entry

Lane Discipline on Dual Lanes & One Way Systems
- Don't Change Lanes on the Late Approach
- Don't Change Lanes whilst negotiating hazard

Traffic Lights
- Before entry (Sequence)
- After entry (Usually at Spiral Roundabouts)

Roundabouts: Turning Left

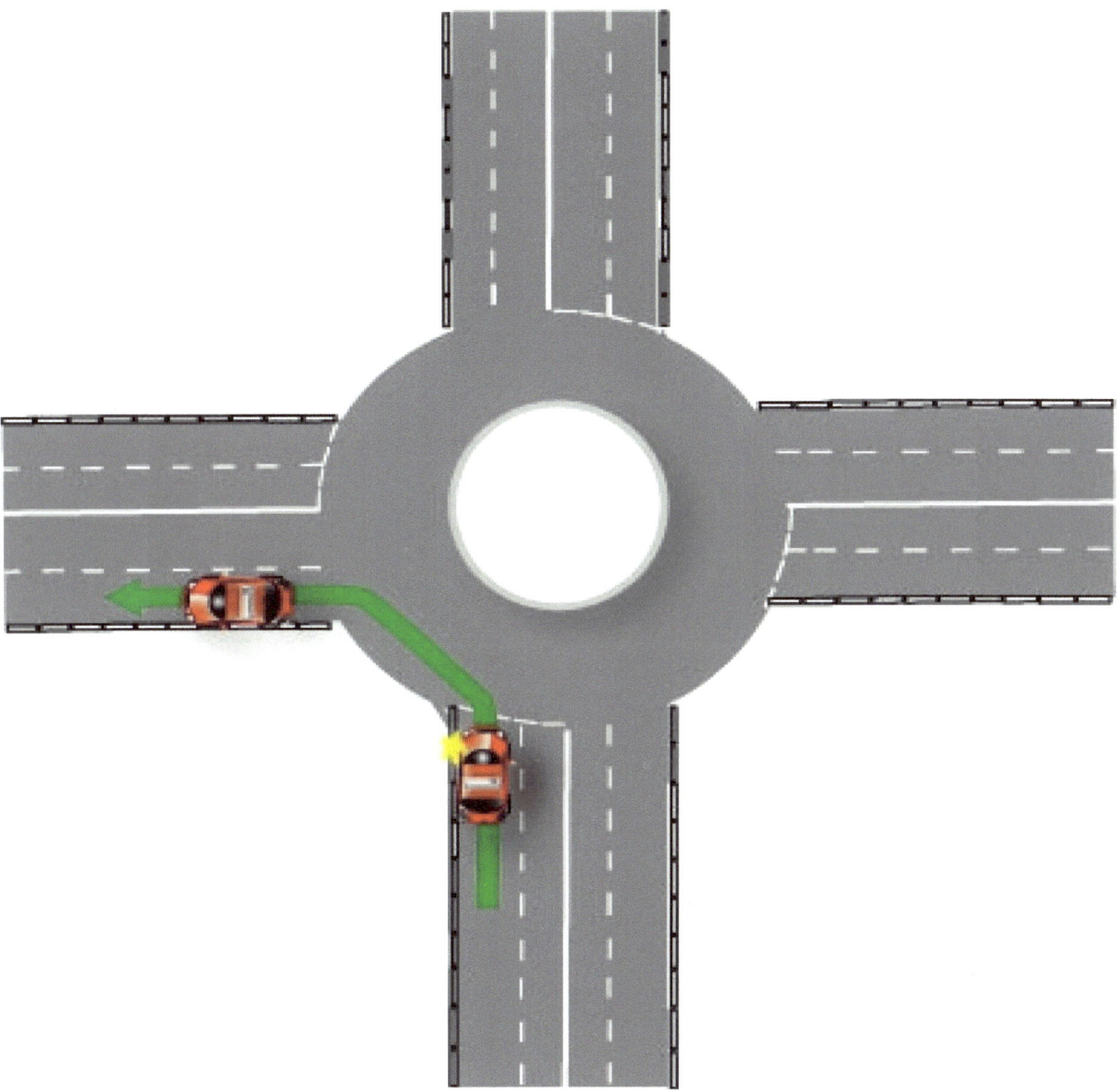

Copyright Bill Bryans, Instructor Training Services, 2009

Roundabouts: Ahead

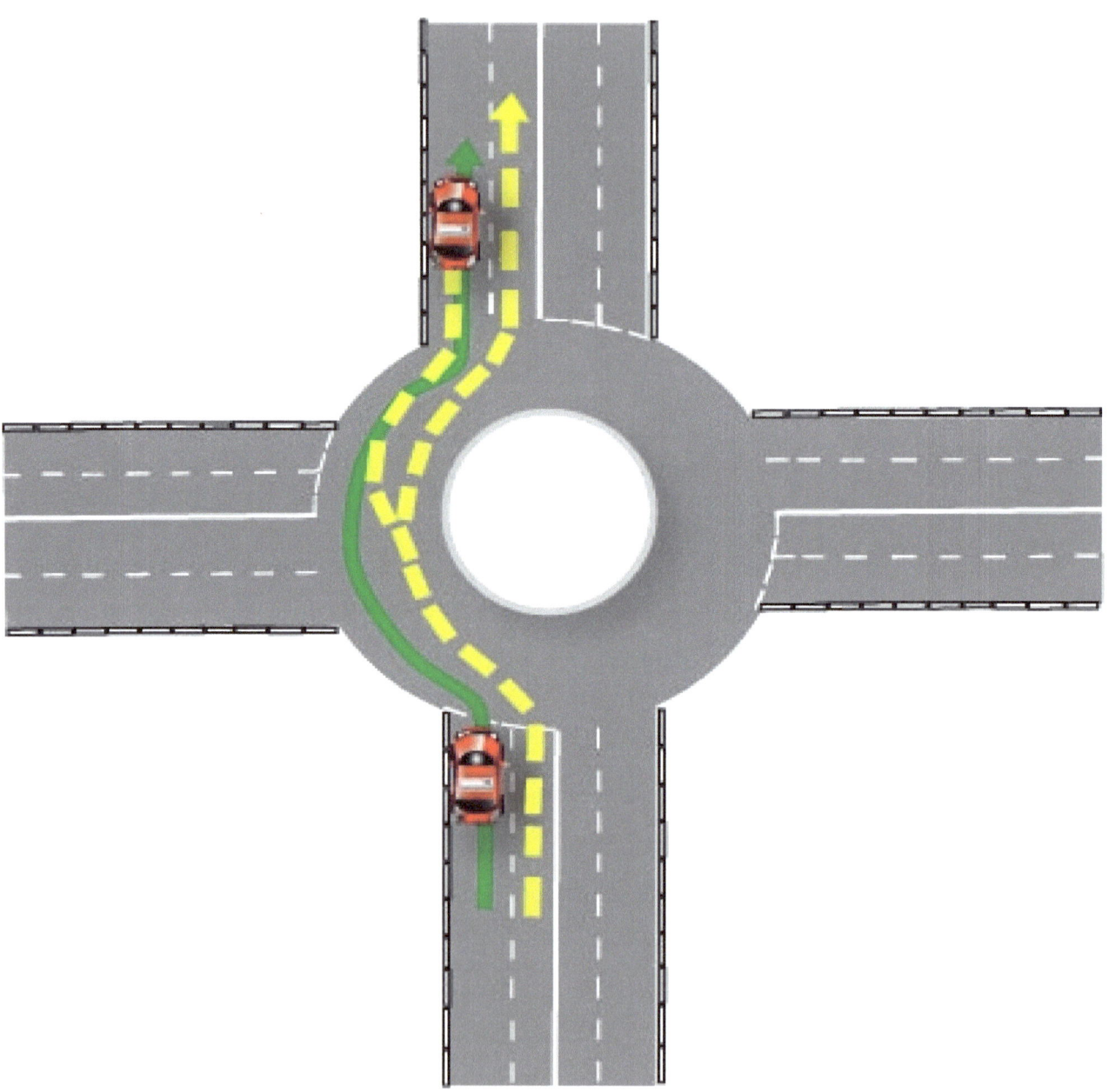

Roundabouts: Turning Right

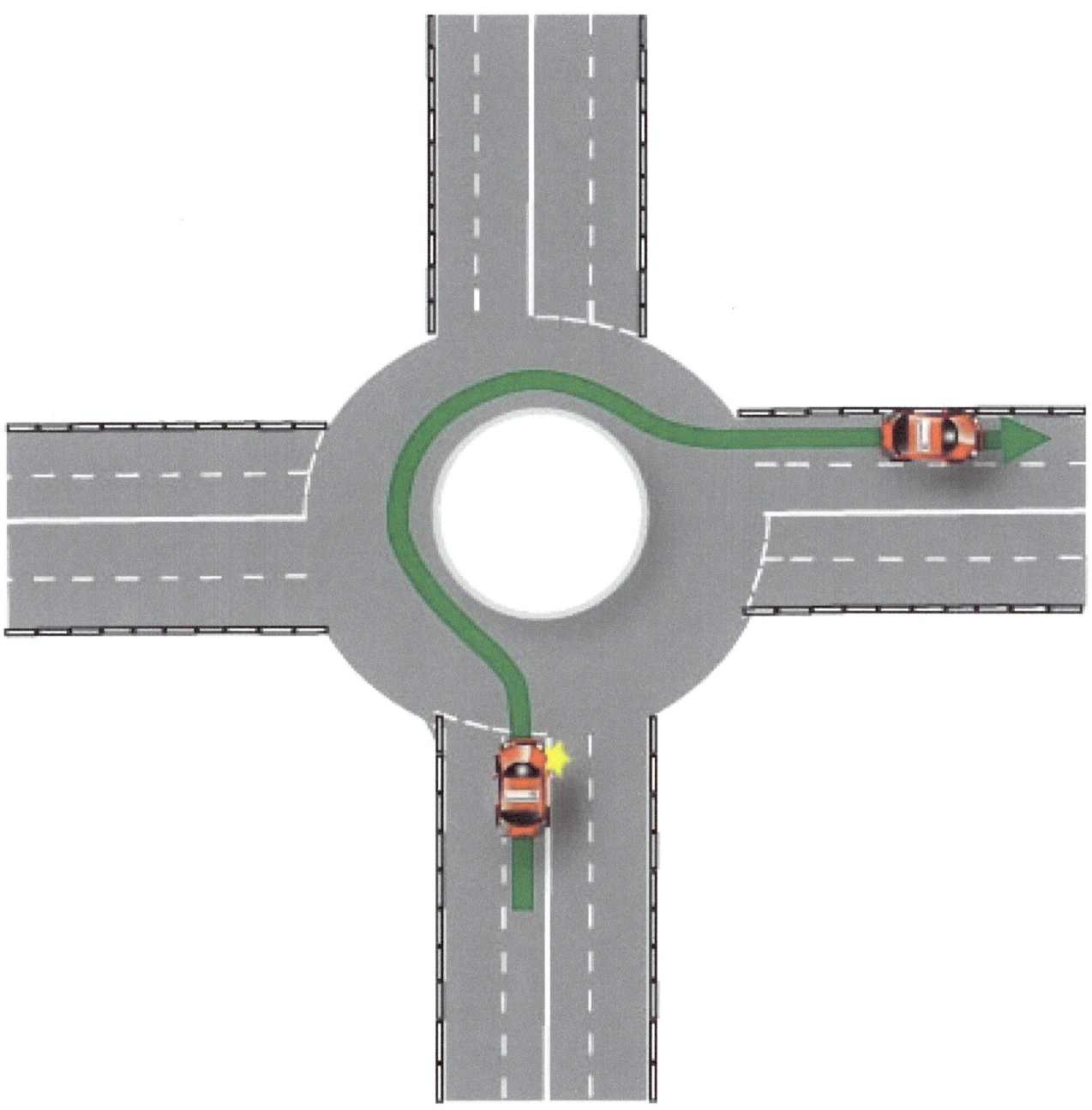

Mini Roundabouts

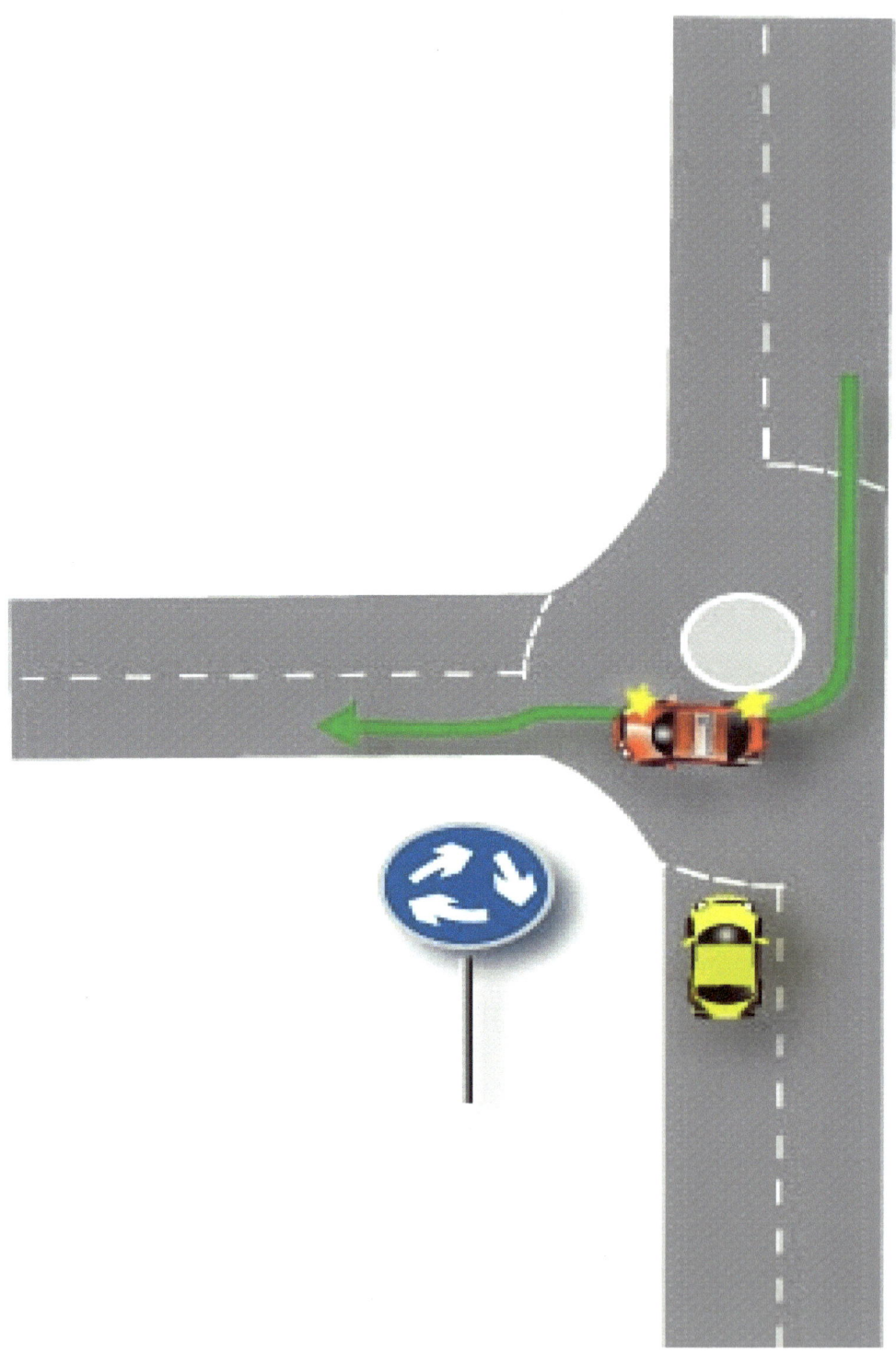

Spiral Roundabouts

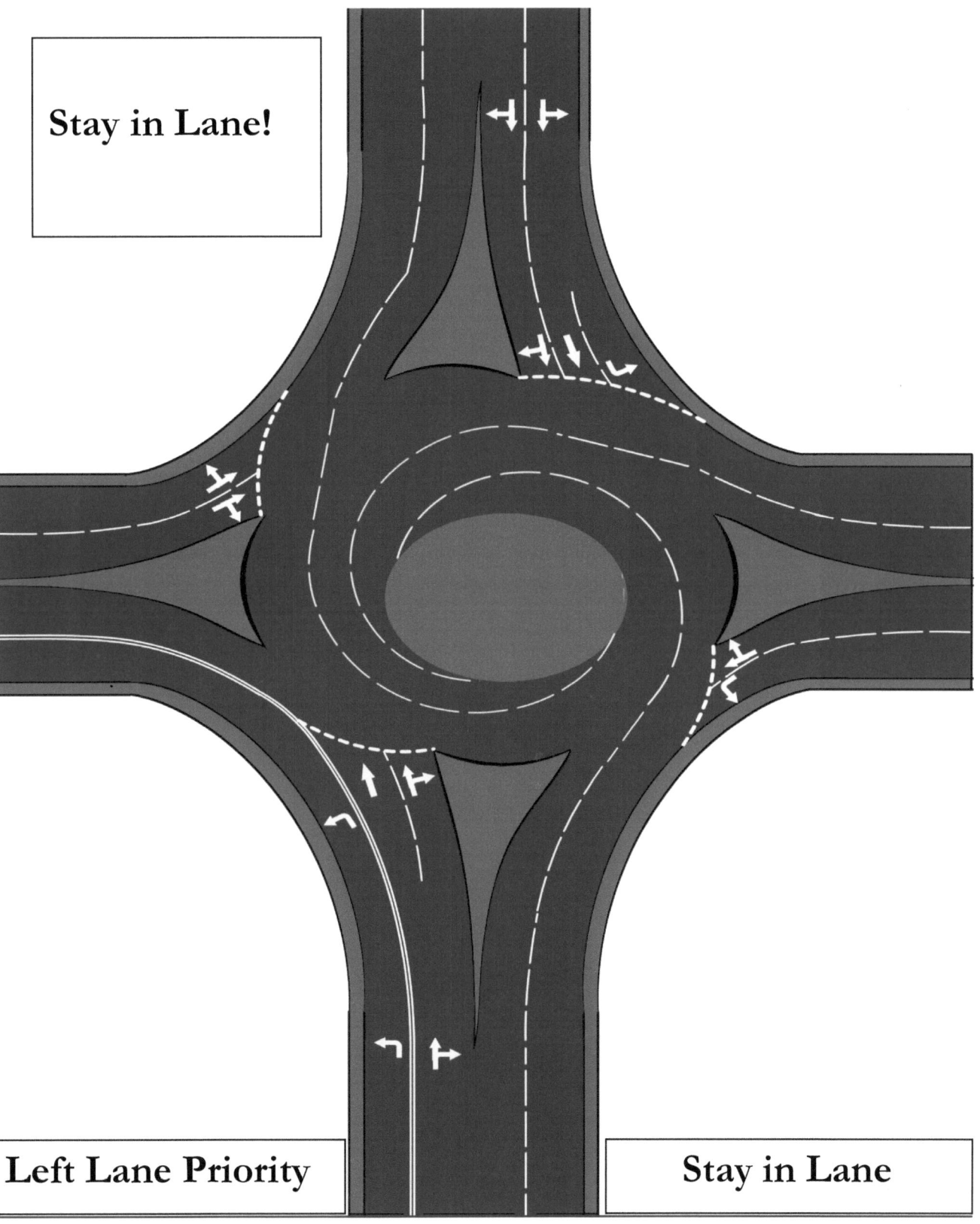

Copyright Bill Bryans, Instructor Training Services, 2009

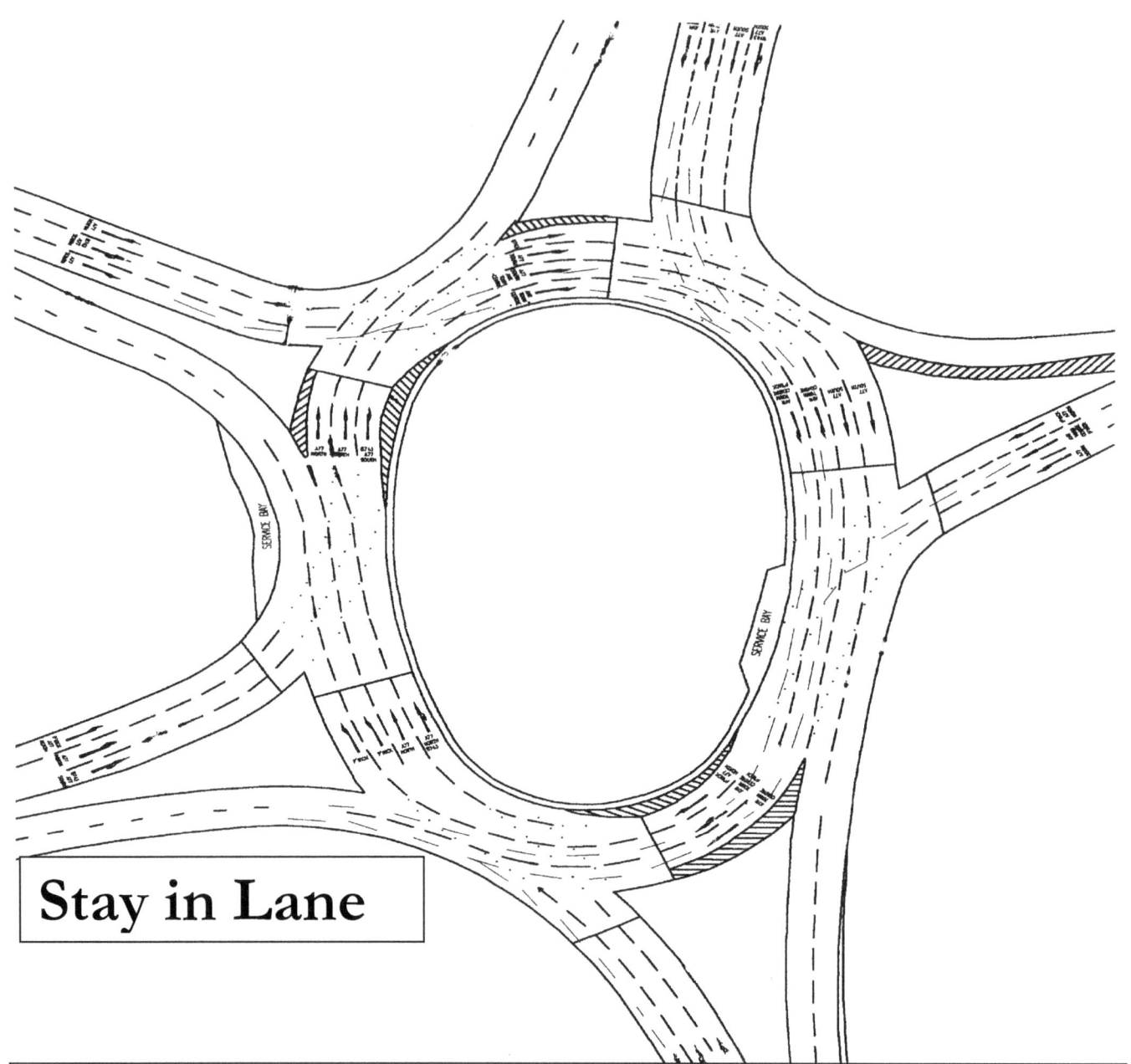

Stay in Lane

Spiral Roundabouts with Traffic lights